CONTINUING THE EDUCATION DEBATE

Also available in the Cassell Education series:

P. Ainley: *Young People Leaving Home*

P. Ainley and M. Corney: *Training for the Future: The Rise and Fall of the Manpower Services Commission*

G. Antonouris and J. Wilson: *Equal Opportunities in Schools*

L. Bash and D. Coulby: *Contradiction and Conflict in Education: The 1988 Act in Action*

N. Bennett and A. Cass: *From Special to Ordinary Schools*

D. E. Bland: *Managing Higher Education*

M. Booth, J. Furlong and M. Wilkin: *Partnership in Initial Teacher Training*

M. Bottery: *The Morality of the School*

L. Burton (ed.): *Gender and Mathematics*

C. Christofi: *Assessment and Profiling in Science*

G. Claxton: *Being a Teacher: A Positive Approach to Change and Stress*

G. Claxton: *Teaching to Learn: A Direction for Education*

D. Coulby and L. Bash: *The Education Reform Act: Competition and Control*

D. Coulby and S. Ward: *The Primary Core National Curriculum*

C. Cullingford (ed.): *The Primary Teacher*

L. B. Curzon: *Teaching in Further Education* (4th edition)

J. Freeman: *Gifted Children Grow Up*

B. Goacher *et al.*: *Policy and Provision for Special Educational Needs*

H. Gray (ed.): *Management Consultancy in Schools*

L. Hall: *Poetry for Life*

J. Nias, G. Southworth and R. Yeomans: *Staff Relationships in the Primary School*

A. Pollard: *The Social World of the Primary School*

J. Sayer and V. Williams (eds): *Schools and External Relations*

B. Spiecker and R. Straughan: *Freedom and Indoctrination in Education: International Perspectives*

R. Straughan: *Beliefs, Behaviour and Education*

H. Thomas: *Education Costs and Performance*

H. Thomas, G. Kirkpatrick and E. Nicholson: *Financial Delegation and the Local Management of Schools*

D. Thyer and J. Maggs: *Teaching Mathematics to Young Children* (3rd edition)

M. Watts: *The Science of Problem-Solving*

J. Wilson: *A New Introduction to Moral Education*

S. Wolfendale (ed.): *Parental Involvement*

Continuing the Education Debate

edited by
Michael Williams
Richard Daugherty
and Frank Banks

CASSELL

Cassell
Villiers House   387 Park Avenue South
41/47 Strand   New York
London   NY 10016–8810
WC2N 5JE

© Department of Education, University College of Swansea, 1992

First published 1992

British Library Cataloguing-in-Publication Data
A catalogue record for this book is available from the British Library.

ISBN 0-304-32616-X (hardback)
   0-304-32614-3 (paperback)

Printed and bound at Page Bros Ltd, Norwich

Contents

Contributors

Frank Banks is a Lecturer in Education in the Department of Education of the University College of Swansea, with special interests in science education and distance learning.

Professor Neville Bennett is Professor of Primary Education and Director of the Centre for Research on Teaching and Learning at the University of Exeter. He has written a number of books focusing on teaching–learning processes in classrooms and teaching competencies of student teachers.

Baroness Tessa Blackstone is Master of Birkbeck College, University of London, and the front bench Opposition spokesman on Education and Science in the House of Lords. Formerly, she was a Chief Officer of the Inner London Education Authority and, before that, Professor of Educational Administration at the University of London Institute of Education.

Rt Hon. Lord Callaghan of Cardiff is a former Prime Minister who had previously been Chancellor of the Exchequer, Home Secretary and Secretary of State for Foreign and Commonwealth Affairs. He was appointed President of the University College of Swansea in 1986.

Richard Daugherty is a Senior Lecturer in the Department of Education of the University College of Swansea. He is Chairman of the Curriculum Council for Wales and was formerly a member of the School Examinations and Assessment Council.

Professor Gareth Elwyn Jones is Research Professor and Head of the Department of Education at the University College of Wales, Aberystwyth, having previously been Reader in Education at the University College of Swansea. He served on both the National Curriculum History Working Group and the National Curriculum History Committee for Wales. He has written or edited sixteen books on the history of education, the teaching of history and the history of Wales.

Rt Hon. John MacGregor is Lord President of the Council and Leader of the House of Commons and a former Secretary of State for Education and Science.

Professor Peter Mittler is Professor of Special Education and Head of the School of Education at the University of Manchester. He has previously been Director of the Hester Adrian Research Centre for the Study of Learning Processes in the Mentally Handicapped and has published widely in the field of special education.

Professor Richard Pring is Professor of Educational Studies and Director of the Department of Educational Studies at the University of Oxford. He is currently editor of the *British Journal of Educational Studies* and his research interests lie in the philosophy of education and education policy.

Professor John Tomlinson has been Director of the Institute of Education at the University of Warwick since 1985. Previously he was Director of Education for Cheshire. He is Chairman of the Council of the Royal Society of Arts and of the recently formed General Teaching Council for England and Wales.

Professor Michael Williams is Professor of Education and Head of the Department of Education at the University College of Swansea. He was formerly Director of the Centre for the In-Service Education of Teachers at the University of Manchester.

Professor Ted Wragg is Professor of Education and Director of the School of Education at the University of Exeter. He has been an active member of a number of national committees concerned with education, has published sixteen books and is a frequent contributor to radio and television programmes, newspapers and journals. He is a regular columnist for the *Times Educational Supplement*.

Preface

Lord Callaghan of Cardiff is the President of the University College of Swansea. It was particularly appropriate therefore that Swansea was the venue for a series of lectures marking the fifteenth anniversary of the Ruskin speech. This speech launched what has become the 'Great Debate' about education in England and Wales. On 18 October 1976, at Ruskin College, Oxford, Lord Callaghan, then Prime Minister, entered what some had called 'the secret garden'.

Exactly fifteen years later, at a one-day conference on 17 October 1992, Lord Callaghan spoke again about education, and he was joined by the Right Honourable John MacGregor, Lord President of the Council and a former Secretary of State for Education, and Professor Ted Wragg of the University of Exeter. These three lectures constitute Part 1 of this volume.

Part 2 comprises the six lectures by distinguished educationalists which followed that conference. They were invited to take stock of particular aspects of education and to predict likely changes over the next fifteen years.

The success of the series owes much to Michael Bristow, who provided essential administrative support for the conference and the lecture series, and to Bronwen Vaughan, secretary to the In Service Unit of the Department of Education, University College of Swansea.

Richard Daugherty and Frank Banks made major contributions to the organization of the series, and played key roles in the production of this book in their meticulous attention to the editing of the text and references.

Finally, I would like to thank Kate Williams for preparing the final manuscript for publication.

MICHAEL WILLIAMS

Chapter 1

Ruskin in Context

Michael Williams

SETTING UP THE DEBATE

Lord Callaghan, writing in his memoirs,[1] recounts how, soon after becoming Prime Minister in 1976, he invited ministers to come and see him individually and without their officials to tell him about their work. He records,

> One of my earliest visitors was Fred Mulley, the Secretary for Education, whom I asked to see me on 21 May, only a few weeks after my appointment. I have always been a convinced believer in the importance of education, as throughout my life I have seen how many doors it could unlock for working-class children who had begun with few other advantages, and I regretted my own lack of a university education. I was also aware of growing concerns among parents about the direction some schools were taking and I was anxious to probe this. (p. 409)

At his meeting he raised four areas of concern with the Secretary of State:

— Was he satisfied with the basic teaching of the three Rs?

— Was the curriculum sufficiently relevant and penetrating for older children in comprehensive schools, especially in the teaching of science and mathematics?

— How did the examination system shape up as a test of achievement?

— What was available for the further education of 16- to 19-year-olds?

Responses to these questions were prepared as a memorandum by July and released to the press. Lord Callaghan recalls how an article in the *Times Educational Supplement*, having suggested that he should not trespass into the sensitive and professional field of education, concluded by 'suspecting selfish political motives and...political demagoguery' (p.410). Rather than taking heed of this advice, Lord Callaghan proceeded on 18 October 1976 to deliver a speech on education at Ruskin College, Oxford.

The occasion for the speech was modest, the laying of a foundation stone for new residential accommodation at the college. The speech itself has become a beacon in the history of post-war education in England and Wales. It brought education into the full light of public debate, giving education a position of prominence on public agendas where it has remained ever since.

In his memoirs, Lord Callaghan summarizes the speech in a single paragraph:

> Teachers, I said, must carry parents with them. Industry complained that some school-leavers did not have the basic tools to do the job and many of our best-trained students from universities and polytechnics had no desire to join industry. Why was this? Why did so many girls abandon science before leaving school, and why were thirty thousand vacancies in science and engineering at universities and polytechnics not taken up, while the humanities courses were full? Were we sacrificing thoroughness and depth in courses in favour of range and diversity? I favoured a basic curriculum with universal standards. 'The essential tools are basic literacy and numeracy; the understanding of how to live and work together; respect for others; and respect for the individual. This means acquiring basic knowledge, skills and reasoning ability; developing lively inquiring minds and an appetite for further knowledge that will last a life-time'. The goal of education was 'to equip children to the best of their ability for a lively constructive place in society and also to fit them to do a job of work' and I emphasised, 'not one or the other, but both'. In today's world there would be fewer jobs for those without skill, and I concluded by asking for a positive response and not a defensive posture in the debate which I hoped would begin. (p. 411)

This bold summary can be enhanced by quoting three passages verbatim from the speech.[2]

> ...there is the unease felt by parents and others about the new informal methods of teaching which seem to produce excellent results when they are in well-qualified hands but are much more dubious when they are not. They seem to be best accepted where strong parent–teacher links exist. There is little wrong with the range and diversity of our courses. But is there sufficient thoroughness and depth in those required in after life to make a living?

> ...There is no virtue in producing socially well-adjusted members of society who are unemployed because they do not have the skills. Nor at the other extreme must they be technically efficient robots. Both of the basic purposes of education require the same essential tools. These are basic literacy, basic numeracy, the understanding of how to live and work together, respect for others, respect for the individual. This means acquiring certain basic knowledge, and skills and reasoning ability. It means developing lively inquiring minds and an appetite for further knowledge that will last a lifetime. It means mitigating as far as possible the disadvantages that may be suffered through poor home conditions or physical or mental handicap. Are we aiming in the right direction in these matters?

> ...Let me repeat some of the fields that need study because they cause concern. There are the methods and aims of informal instruction; the strong case for the so-called 'core curriculum' of basic knowledge; next, what is the proper way of monitoring the use of resources in order to maintain a proper national standard of performance; then there is the role of the Inspectorate in relation to national standards; and there is the need to improve relations between industry and education.

In these quotations are embedded the principal items that framed the 'Great Debate' which was to follow. To these items we can add brief references made in the speech to the examination system in secondary schools, with particular reference to the needs of less academic students staying at school beyond the age of 16. There was also a brief reference to the anticipated Taylor Committee Report on the government and management of schools.

This was a comprehensive agenda which led, in the autumn of 1976, to meetings between the Secretaries of State for Education and Science and for Wales and a number of industrial and educational organizations at which an unpublished paper outlining possible issues for consideration was discussed. There followed a second stage of consultation in February and March 1977 which consisted of eight regional conferences. For these conferences four main topics were chosen for debate: the school curriculum; the assessment of standards; the education and training of teachers; school and working life. For the Welsh conference the place of the Welsh language in the schools of Wales was added to the list. The central issues for each item on the list were spelled out in a background paper prepared by the Department of Education and Science (1977).[3] It was this paper, closely tied to the Ruskin speech, which launched what became the 'Great Debate'.

DEBATING THE ISSUES

In the years since 1976 there has been a regular flow of documents concerned with education. They have emanated from the Department of Education and Science (DES), the Welsh Office, Her Majesty's Inspectorate (HMI), local education authorities (LEAs), teacher unions, professional associations, examination boards, subject associations and many other national, regional and local bodies. Some were directed at the education service, others were written for a broader audience. Many invited responses, and preparing responses to centrally initiated documents has become part of the politicization of many bodies which had previously had little engagement with central government agencies.

Since 1976 the education system in England and Wales has experienced radical transformations in structures and processes. The triangular relationship between the Department of Education and Science/Welsh Office, the LEAs and the teachers has changed as the centre has acquired more functions at the expense of LEA and teacher autonomy. Virtually all aspects of the education system have been reviewed in a piecemeal way so that by 1992 we can see primary education, secondary education, tertiary and further education, teacher education, adult education and higher education all subject to major upheavals. In this book we shall focus our attention on the primary, secondary and tertiary phases but in so doing we are conscious of the changes taking place elsewhere in the system, changes which interact to influence the total picture. Two principal structures which have been transformed since 1976 are the curriculum and management of primary and secondary schools.

CURRICULUM

The curriculum was the focus of two HMI survey reports which appeared in 1978[4] and 1979.[5] The former identified the strengths and weaknesses of curriculum and teaching in primary schools. It pointed to the inadequate attention given to such subjects as geography, history and science and raised questions about the standards achieved by pupils in the basic skills of reading and writing.

The second report (DES, 1979) was critical of the secondary school curriculum, which was seen to lack a rationale appropriate for comprehensive schools. The shortage of specialist teaching in key curriculum subjects was highlighted. What was particularly striking was the lack of a common curriculum and the poor quality of guidance given to pupils as they made subject and course choices at the age of 14.

Alongside these surveys should be set the Warnock Report[6] published in 1978. Here it was asserted that one in five pupils had learning difficulties at any one time. It introduced the practice of 'statementing' pupils with special educational needs. This report was an important milestone in the provision of appropriate education for these pupils. It was comprehensive in its coverage, calling for a more positive approach to providing the appropriate help for pupils assessed as having special educational needs, which the Committee saw as extending beyond the particular disabilities which a child may be judged to have to include all those factors which have a bearing on his or her educational progress. The Education Act of 1981 provided the legal framework for changes in the 1980s. Considerable progress has been made in the provision of special schools and the integration of pupils with special needs into ordinary schools. We recognized the importance of the issue when we invited Professor Peter Mittler to participate in this lecture series.

The debate about the curriculum, started in the Ruskin speech, moved quickly through discussions about a common curriculum[7] and a core curriculum[8] with a parallel focus on subjects and curriculum areas stimulated by the Curriculum Matters Series written by HMI.

By 1985 the DES was ready to take stock of these discussions, together with the specialist Cockcroft Report on mathematics (1982)[9] and the Swann Report on the education of children of minority groups (1985),[10] which added to the earlier report on language, the Bullock Report (1975).[11] In the White Paper *Better Schools*[12] the DES stated its intention to raise standards at all levels of ability and to secure the best possible returns from the resources invested in education. It was asserted that the government would take the lead in promoting national agreement about the purposes and content of the curriculum. Here was the foundation for the curriculum proposals incorporated into the Education Reform Act of 1988. This Act embodied a statutory National Curriculum introducing attainment targets and programmes of study for pupils in newly defined key stages. These were for pupils in state schools in the period of compulsory schooling. A rolling programme for introducing ten subjects in England and eleven subjects in Wales as a common, compulsory curriculum is now being implemented. Alongside the introduction of National Curriculum foundation subjects has come experimentation with national tests to be taken by pupils at the end of each of the four key stages. It is possible to trace the development from the Ruskin speech to the imposition of the National Curriculum.

SCHOOL ORGANIZATION AND MANAGEMENT

The recent history of the school curriculum is distinguished by the rapid movement towards a centrally regulated, statutory National Curriculum. In contrast to this centralized system for the curriculum must be placed the centrally directed, legally bound, move to decentralize the control of schools in the state sector. Many of the functions and responsibilities of local education authorities, with particular reference to budgets and resource allocation, have been delegated to the governing bodies of individual schools. Individual schools have become cost centres and are becoming accustomed to the specification of performance indicators which are of considerable importance in the drafting of school plans and policies. The requirement that schools publish information for parents and, in this information, the inclusion of test results for pupils at the various key stages, has promoted the ethos of competition to which schools have rapidly become sensitized. For financial reasons schools must compete for pupils and a nationally introduced policy of open enrolment has reinforced the need for schools to consider carefully the strategies they employ for marketing themselves.

Alongside the increased autonomy of individual schools as cost centres and management units must be set the loss of responsibilities and functions of LEAs. This is evident in the changed functional relationship between LEAs and the schools within their boundaries. It is also evident in the changing definitions of the role of LEA advisers, as inspecting and monitoring become more significant than their teacher support and professional development functions.

It is worth noting that in the time of the Great Debate an important structural change has been the replacement of the Schools Council for Curriculum and Examinations—a body set up to bring together the DES/Welsh Office, LEAs and teachers—by, initially the School Curriculum Development Committee (SCDC) and the Secondary Examinations Council (SEC), and more recently the National Curriculum Council (NCC) in England, the Curriculum Council for Wales (CCW), and the School Examinations and Assessment Council (SEAC) for England and Wales.

Accompanying these structural changes for curriculum and examinations has been the reform of secondary school examinations. In particular the General Certificate of Education (GCE) and the Certificate of Secondary Education (CSE) have been replaced by a unitary General Certificate of Secondary Education (GCSE). Examinations for this new award have been designed to meet national criteria and, for the administration of the new examination, there is a regional grouping of examination boards. Changes have also occurred in examinations in the immediate post-16 phase of education. We have witnessed the introduction of the AS Levels, the Certificate of Pre-Vocational Education and BTEC in courses for 16- to 19-year-olds. In 1992 the reform of this sector remains an area of debate and contention. Bridging the gap between compulsory schooling and the post-16 phase has been the Technical and Vocational Education Initiative (TVEI) introduced by the Manpower Services Commission, since reorganized, in 1983.

THE DEBATE CONTINUES

What emerges from this brief introductory sketch is the image of an educational system in ferment. There have been numerous initiatives, important reports, discussion documents galore and highly significant legislation. Alongside these largely centralized activities must be set the changes set in motion by local education authorities and individual schools.

Despite all this change there is still a major concern for educational progress. In 1990, in his presidential address to the British Association meeting in Swansea, Sir Claus Moser warned that '...this country is now in danger of becoming one of the least adequately educated of all the advanced nations—with serious consequences for its future, socially, economically, technologically and culturally.'[13] He urged a complete review of education, 'all-embracing, visionary yet realistic', and highlighted fourteen issues which required attention.

It was particularly fitting that Swansea should be the location for the series of lectures reported in this book. Lord Callaghan, as President of the University College of Swansea, was warm in his response to the suggestion that we should mount a series of lectures under the title 'Continuing the Great Debate'. We were able to bring together colleagues who are experts in the fields of primary, secondary, tertiary and special education to present a series of lectures.

The series began with a one day conference held at the Taliesin Theatre on 18 October 1992. Lord Callaghan made the first presentation and he was followed onto the platform by the Right Honourable John MacGregor, a former Secretary of State for Education and Science, and Professor Ted Wragg. Their speeches form Part 1 of this book.

In Part 2 we present the lectures given in the series which followed the conference. They were delivered at the Department of Education of the University College of Swansea on Friday evenings in the autumn term. Each lecturer was asked to review the current educational scene from a particular perspective and then reflect on how they perceived educational changes over the next fifteen years. They were urged to consider the continuation of the education debate in the light of current and anticipated pressures for reform and change. The chapters in Part 2 have been written as academic papers though the quality of the spoken word has not been lost in their presentation.

NOTES

1.   Callaghan, J. (1987) *Time and Chance*. London: Collins.
2.   Callaghan, J. (1976) 'Towards a national debate', reprinted in *Education*, 22 October 1976, pp. 332-3.
3.   DES (1977) *Educating Our Children: Four Subjects for Debate*. London: DES.
4.   DES (1978) *Primary Education in England*. London: HMSO.
5.   DES (1979) *Aspects of Secondary Education in England*. London: HMSO.
6.   DES (1978) *Report of the Committee of Enquiry into the Education of Handicapped Children and Young People: Special Educational Needs* (The Warnock Report). London: HMSO.
7.   DES (1977) *Curriculum 11-16, Working Papers by HM Inspectorate: A Contribution to Current Debate*. London: DES.
8.   DES (1980) *A Framework for the School Curriculum*. London: DES.
9.   DES (1982) *A Report of the Committee of Enquiry into the Teaching of Mathematics in Schools in England and Wales: Mathematics Counts* (The Cockcroft Report). London: HMSO.
10. DES (1985) *Report of the Committee of Enquiry into Education of Children of Ethnic Minority Groups. Education for All* (The Swann Report). London: HMSO.
11. DES (1975) *A Language for Life* (The Bullock Report). London: HMSO.
12. HMSO (1985) *Better Schools*, White Paper. London: HMSO.
13. Moser, C. (1990) *Our Need for an Informed Society*, Presidential Address, British Association, London, p. 14.

Part 1

Chapter 2

The Education Debate I

The Rt Hon. Lord Callaghan of Cardiff, KG

I am very honoured that the Department of Education of Swansea University College should hold a conference to mark the anniversary of the launch of the Great Debate on Britain's educational aims and methods which took place at Ruskin College, Oxford on 18 October 1976, exactly fifteen years ago today.

Of all the countless speeches I have delivered in a long political life, the Ruskin speech is the one that is best remembered, and even today I have to maintain a small stock to meet requests for copies from students and others. It attracted wide publicity, much more than I had anticipated, because it touched a sensitive spot among parents and employers.

By some of the educational elite it was thought to be an unseemly intrusion of the Prime Minister to poke his nose into educational matters and stir up trouble on matters best left to those who know most. I am glad to say that this attitude has now mostly gone by the board, although occasionally there are faint echoes of it. The effect at the time was like a stone dislodged by the mountaineer's foot which, rolling down the mountain side, precipitates an avalanche. Since then, the debate on aims and methods, structure and content has hardly stopped and so on this occasion there is no danger of reproof now that I once again dip my toe in the educational pool.

In 1976 I asked what were the educational practices that were causing criticism among parents and employers? Was it that child-centred informal instruction was being misunderstood or misused, and was thoroughness being sacrificed by schools in pursuit of diversity? Why did some school-leavers lack the basic tools to do a job when they left school? Why did so many girls abandon science even before leaving school? On the other hand, was the curriculum sufficiently demanding? And, addressing a wider audience than the schools, I asked why did industry rank so low in young people's preference for careers? I suggested the introduction of basic curriculum (not, let me emphasize, a straitjacket) with national standards of performance to ensure basic literacy and numeracy. The goal, I said, should be to equip children to the best of their ability for a lively, constructive place in society, and at the same time to fit them to do a job of work. 'Not one or the other,' I emphasized, 'but both'.

The first thing to note is that, although both my Government and those of my successors have attempted to answer some of these questions, yet, as soon as they were removed from the agenda, others took their place. Fifteen years later the debate has still not ended. Indeed the expression of public concern is even more deep-seated than it was fifteen years ago. It was Prince Charles who recently used the occasion of a Shakespeare birthday lecture to call attention to the unsatisfactory state of nursery education, to deplore the number of children who leave school with no significant qualifications, and to urge that education be given number one priority. During this year there have been major debates in both Houses of Parliament which have called for significant changes in the priorities, structure and content of education.

The Senior Chief Inspector of Schools tells us that in English schools some 30 per cent of lessons were judged to be poor, or very poor, and in the most scathing criticism of all, Sir Claus Moser in his Presidential Address to the British Association for the Advancement of Science[1] uttered a stark warning. This country 'is now in danger of becoming one of the least adequately educated of all the advanced nations'. He called for a leap forward 'in the quality and vision of...the educational goals we set ourselves'.

So fifteen years later, after six Secretaries of State and five new Education Acts, that is the verdict on the past and the horrid forecast for the future. And yet, there has been such a positive torrent of legislation with so much change in methods, content and structure, that teachers complain of 'innovation fatigue'.

School governing bodies have been reformed to give more power to parents, and schools' admissions policy changed to increase choice. 'O' Levels and CSE disappeared to be replaced by GCSE, and new Training and Enterprise Councils were established to oversee and improve technical, vocational and business training. In 1988, the Government introduced the biggest reforms since the 1944 Act, including schools managing their own budgets, standard testing and, of course, the National Curriculum. The performance of teachers is to be appraised every two years, and for the future we are promised—or threatened—that the Secretary of State's objective will be to persuade the majority of schools to opt out of the Local Education Authority system.

It has been obvious that many of the changes of the last decade have been inspired as much by the Government's ideology—a dislike of local government, a disrespect for those working in the public services, a fixed idea that all problems can be solved by privatization—as by a serious attempt to get to the root of the nation's educational shortcomings.

Too little attempt was made in the early years to enlist the support of educationalists for the changes, and much of the change has been *ad hoc*, lacking coherence or continuity. Nevertheless there are genuine improvements to record. More 16-year-olds are staying on at school, the argument about child-centred education is finding a point of balance, a national curriculum is coming into existence with measurable standards, the GCSE is a success, there is better understanding between industry and education, and education itself has a much higher public profile—even if the reason is that the public is concerned because it is not yet good enough.

It is also a hopeful sign that there is some agreement on objectives, even if not on means, between the Government and the Opposition about the newest proposals for education and training of the 16- to 19-year-olds, so that some accommodation may not be out of reach.

But public dissatisfaction is more general, and falls into two categories. First, there is Sir Claus Moser's alarm about Britain's national prospects, and his fear that our level of education for the average child and in particular our ignorance of science and technology in a rapidly changing competitive world will have 'serious consequences for Britain's future, socially, economically, technologically and culturally'.

The second criticism is that despite real improvement in educational attainments since the Ruskin speech, too many children at the lower end of the educational range leave school having achieved less than they are capable of.

Sir John Cassels, the Director of the newly formed National Commission on Education under the Chairmanship of Lord Walton of Detchant put it this way: our system 'educated to a high level and a good standard a rather small proportion of each age group while neglecting the needs and capabilities of a good many of the rest'.[2]

This general indictment is coupled with more specific charges—not enough teachers, too poorly paid, one in five science teachers lacking the knowledge to teach their subjects, not enough mathematicians, insufficient resources. These are but some of them.

As in many other industrialized countries, more 16-year-olds are staying at school than fifteen years ago. But these others have gone ahead faster than we have, so, taking the 16–18 groups as a whole, no more than 37 per cent of our young people are receiving full-time education, whilst in Japan and the United States the comparable figure is 85 per cent or more. Several other of our industrial competitors have more than 70 per cent of 16- to 18-year-olds in full time education, twice as many as in Britain. At 19 years of age, the figures are Britain 15 per cent, the United States 48 per cent.

It used to be said that Britain had three native resources only—coal, fish and brains. Regrettably the once great coal industry is but a shrunken pygmy, the Spanish armada is catching our fish, and we still have not discovered how to make the best use of our brains.

We live in a world in which the numbers of semi-skilled and unskilled jobs are declining and will continue to do so. There will be little place in the twenty-first century for a semi-literate and semi-numerate population, for those without skilled qualifications—academic or vocational. It would be a betrayal to allow, by default or wilful neglect, this fate to overtake our people.

A welcome beginning to remedy this has been made with the introduction of the Technical and Vocational Education Initiative (the TVEI). Its focus on science and technology, the positive support it gives to industry and commerce, and its emphasis on 'real world' problems, have given a new relevance to the school curriculum for some of the disaffected 14- to 16-year-olds.

Recently the Government has published its latest proposals, *Education and Training for the 21st Century*,[3] sponsored by three separate Departments (Education, Employment and Wales). Let me say, in passing, that I believe this division of responsibility between departments for the 16- to 19-year-olds, although awkward, is inevitable. It makes for overlapping difficulties, of course, but no machinery of government change, for example by giving responsibility to a single department, would overcome them. Most likely it would take away one set of difficulties only to replace them by another.

I welcome the Government's declared objective to end the artificial divide between academic and vocational qualifications. If it succeeds, as it must do if Britain is to prosper, we shall have overcome at long last the separation of young people at age 16 into two groups, one of which has been deemed superior to the other and on which much more care and attention has been lavished. But let no one doubt the difficulty of changing both the perception and the reality.

Success will require three conditions to be satisfied. Standards will have to be the same for all qualifications at the same stage of advancement; more resources will have to be made available; and the attention of employers will have to be captured and then harnessed to a system which they understand and accept as the best way to ensure the transition from school to work.

The Government's proposed method is to make generally available from age 16 a new Certificate to be called a National Vocational Qualification (NVQ). It will be based on standards laid down by employers, and set in a framework of graduated levels of attainment which can be attained at various stages in a person's career. The Government's intention is that it should be of equal standing with academic qualifications at the same level. Will it be so? In particular, how will it stand up against the A-Level examination, long regarded as the essential test of whether a candidate is fit to enter university?

The Prime Minister has made this the litmus test in his introduction to the new proposals. A-Levels will remain the benchmark of academic excellence. The hope is to ensure equal esteem for the new National Vocational Qualifications, through a new system of Ordinary and Advanced Diplomas to be awarded for success in either A-Levels or NVQs. The details of the scheme are the subject of consultation, so this is the appropriate moment to comment.

The Government's proposals are an improvement on the existing position but I have my doubts as to whether they are sufficiently radical to ensure equal esteem for NVQs and A-Levels.

A-Levels are a one-time examination taken at the end of an intensive two-year course in the sixth form. Candidates either fail or succeed, and if they fail they think it is the end of the road. For university entry it is all or nothing. NVQs on the other hand will be cumulative. Young people will reach the qualifying level one step at a time and at various stages in their careers and then pass on to the next phase. The objective is that those who choose the NVQ route will be perceived to have the same status as those who follow the A-Level route.

There must be serious doubt that we shall hit that target as long as A-Levels are accepted and proclaimed as the 'benchmarks of success'. It is difficult to understand the Government's determination to cling to them when there is widespread dissatisfaction in academic circles and among Government advisers with their present range and operation.

The Government should think again and be more radical. For example, why not introduce a single advanced award at age 18 or 19, through a unified system of education and training that would involve both schools and employers and embrace existing A-Levels and vocational awards. The Institute for Public Policy Research have put forward some interesting proposals for such a scheme in their document *A British Baccalaureat* [4] that would repay further scrutiny. Our aim must be to avoid the exclusiveness of A-Levels, the narrowness of vocational qualifications, and the lack of credibility in records of achievement.

I urge that some such scheme be devised. It might at long last enable Britain to rid itself of the two cultures which create a gulf between those who are educated to know and understand and those who are educated to create and do.

There is no secret about how to achieve a better educated nation. Good teachers are the key to well educated pupils. Yet Britain is short of teachers and not all of those in post have adequate qualifications. It is said that their morale is not high; their pay is too low; their status has been undermined by changes in society which makes their tasks more difficult; they feel overworked; and their career development is inadequate. There is a lot of truth in this dismal catalogue, but, despite the shortcomings, I find wherever I go bands of dedicated men and women who care for their charges and whose professional pride overcomes their personal disappointments.

There is much good teaching and some high standards in many of our schools. But not in all. It is fruitless to argue whether today's standards are higher or lower than in the past, although many competent observers will agree that they are higher than they used to be. Lord Annan has pointed out that during the years of National Service nearly 20 per cent of those entering the Armed Forces were illiterate. But whether higher or not is beside the point. The nub of the matter is that Britain's educational standards for the majority of school leavers urgently need to be raised if we are to approach the twenty-first century with confidence in our future as a leading industrial nation. We are wasting too much individual talent, and too many are underachieving. To do better we shall have to begin with the teachers—the key to success. Their self-esteem matters.

They must be given the confidence that they are professionally respected and trusted, and that they will be properly remunerated with a planned career. They must feel fully involved in planning the changes that result from the pressure of innovation. The other side of the coin is that they be less defensive when those outside the profession propose change.

We must not repeat the errors of the 1980s made by both sides, which led teachers to feel that their practical experience was overlooked in planning massive changes, some of which, like the National Curriculum, needed second thoughts, and others, like the tests, left them submerged under a mountain of paper. The remuneration aspect of this package may be improved by the Government's decision to establish a National Pay Review Body—a development that I welcome.

As Prime Minister, I both appointed such bodies and handled their recommendations. My experience was that their members, who were usually independently minded people, took a broad view of their responsibilities, were open to submissions from both sides, were sympathetic to those whose claims they were considering, and backed up their conclusions and recommendations with well reasoned arguments. Because of this it is morally more difficult for a government to override their recommendations and there is a strong presumption that it will not do so except in a dire emergency. The worst a government usually does is to defer the implementation of a report or to implement it by instalments.

However, I have a reservation about the intention that the Teachers' Pay Review Body shall also have responsibility to adjudicate on teachers' duties and working time. These are internal matters which even more than pay fixing require direct and detailed knowledge of conditions at the coalface. Only the principal parties have that detailed understanding, and my experience is that such matters require flexibility and compromise and are best handled by direct negotiation and agreement, rather than by judgements handed down. I recommend another think about this.

For related but rather different reasons, I question whether it was wise for Mr Baker to introduce a teachers' contract which stipulates the exact number of hours a teacher is required to work. That runs against the grain of teaching as a profession and may lead to the minimum number of hours becoming the maximum for some staff. I seem to remember that many teachers prided themselves on working whatever hours the job needed. I am sure they do still, and, although the contract may make no difference to their performance, nevertheless it can forfeit a certain goodwill. Has the contract had any adverse effect on teachers being willing to give their time, as they did in the past, to extra-curricular activities? Leisure pursuits and games are an important part of absorbing a culture and a rounded education, yet in a number of quarters, from cricket to chess, I hear complaints that state schools are quietly dropping such activities. If the contract is not the cause, is this the result of an overcrowded National Curriculum?

Way back in 1976 it was far from my thoughts when I proposed a National Curriculum that it should turn into a statutory straitjacket. The clamp will have to be loosened. Everything is subject to change—even the Statutory Orders of the Secretary of State for Education, and some subjects will be impossible to pin down. Innovations must not be strangled; there must be space for experiment and unorthodoxy in the classroom. The run of the mill will get by through teaching learning packages out of textbooks prepared for the purpose—and very useful some will be. But it would be a sad day if the imaginative teacher, the man or woman who awakens ideas and thoughts beyond the child's experience, and leaves a lasting impression in the hearer's mind, were ever to be cramped or confined by a rigid National Curriculum backed by law, and perhaps even challenged in the courts by perverse interests. I do not anticipate this will happen, but the teaching profession will have to be on guard against such a development.

'Child-centred' education was a source of controversy in 1976, but I doubt that the Ruskin speech inflamed that dispute which was already well alight before I spoke. It seemed to me then that the methods had not been properly understood or digested by some of the practitioners, but now fifteen years later, I hope I am right in believing that a better balance has been struck between the 'child-centred' radicals and the traditionalists. It is time that the controversy was put to sleep.

There are some interesting new teacher training initiatives which I hope will be widely extended, and I firmly believe that the art of successful teaching comes with practice in the classroom quite as much as from precept. 'An ounce of practice...' Once again it is a matter of establishing the right balance. Understanding how children learn is an important tool as is the ability to reflect critically on teaching technique—analysing what 'works' and what is less successful—but I wonder whether some theoretical study of methods, development of pastoral skills and such matters would not be likely to be more relevant later in the teacher's career when practical experience has been gained. Opportunities for further training, following a proper induction programme, should be part of normal career development. This is a matter which is still inadequately treated despite the recommendations of the James Report some twenty years ago. By no means will every teacher wish to become a headteacher if that means giving up all teaching for full-time administration, managing the budget, soothing the governors, engaging and dismissing staff, and so on.

With the massive changes now in progress this is pre-eminently the moment to cap them by establishing a standing General Teaching Council, to set professional standards, which should include training and retraining, and also qualifications, selection, planned secondments to and from industry and perhaps other matters. The majority of members should of course be members of the teaching profession, but the Council would be strengthened by the addition of a number of lay members drawn from a wider circle. The General Medical Council for example, now includes lay members nominated by the Lord President of the Council. The Bar Council co-opts lay members on to its professional standards and disciplinary committees. The General Teaching Council would have a higher public standing if it did the same. Side by side with the National Review Body already in place, there would then be two powerful bodies acting in parallel and bringing many aspects of a teacher's life under their two umbrellas. This could, within five years, transform teachers' morale, restore their self-esteem and give the profession a renewed respect in the eyes of the public. Let me repeat. Good teachers are the key to higher standards.

In the fifteen years since Ruskin some important bits of Britain's educational strategy have shown improvement. There are many good schools, and if all schools were up to their standard we should have little to fear—but they are not. Too many 16-year-olds leave school alienated from its influence and with little or no desire to continue learning. Unless we devise a firm structure of continued education and training to enable them to make a successful transition from school to work, the potential capability of many 16- to 19-year-olds will never be fulfilled.

Reliance on shibboleths like the 'discipline of the market-place' and the 'engine of competition' have little relevance to the educational needs of the future, and even less to the principle of equality and opportunity for all our children. On the contrary, if the Secretary for Education gets his way and cajoles or bribes most schools to opt out of the system he will widen the educational divide and leave swathes of children undereducated.

We are very far from the ideal that all our children should have the same access to learning and similar opportunities and facilities to follow their studies. Too often so called 'bad' schools are no more than the mirror image of the social differences in our society. They are often found where unemployment is highest, the maximum squalor exists, there is the greatest poverty, the lowest aspiration, the least hope and expectation of something better from life. How do you motivate a 16-year-old from such a background to continue seriously with education and training if he has little or no expectation of a job at the end of it?

Mr Tebbit, in his usual combative style, carries his dogmatic ideology beyond the edge of reason when he declares that we should be free to choose the worst. He knows what conditions can be found in some cities and he surely cannot believe that his doctrine should apply to education in towns and cities where our children have no realistic choice and small opportunity.

Consider two schools in a city not a thousand miles from here. One serves a residential area, carefully tended gardens, well furnished homes, a professional community. The other is the gathering ground for an old estate, high unemployment, petty crime, vandalism and graffiti. From February to June 1991, average daily attendance at the first school was 93 per cent. In the second, no more than 69 per cent. How relevant to the educational problems of the second school will 'competition', 'choice', the 'discipline of the market-place' be? Does anyone seriously expect that in this area parents will act quickly to transfer their children to the 'good' school, until the 'bad' is so weakened by loss of numbers that it withers away? I simply do not believe it.

I know that some schools perform better than their neighbours although both have similar intakes of children and similar resources, but the so-called league tables of performance will not remedy this. They may highlight the differences between schools, but will be too crude to identify the causes or to cure the weaknesses. Recognizing this, the Labour Party has proposed that a Standards Commission should assume responsibility for investigating and taking whatever action is required to improve these schools. Another method might be to give the new General Teaching Council additional powers to take such problems under its wing, and in this way avoid a proliferation of bureaucracies.

What is certain is that atomizing the local schools system, with a majority of schools being cajoled into opting out, will not close the gap but will widen it. We cannot permit the creation of educational ghettos which would result in the present gap between social groups becoming a chasm with catastrophic consequences for a divided society.

Education has a dual purpose. It is vital for the individual child, but it is also essential for a society that hopes to thrive in the modern competitive world. 'Choice' and 'competition' are the current vogue words to achieve these ends. By themselves they will fail unless the unfashionable banners of 'community' and 'co-operation' are raised once again.

The 1980s was a decade in which huge emphasis was placed on the virtues of self help and individualism, coupled with attacks on the notion of community welfare for the common uplift. Long-held values are being modified and are changing at a rapid pace, with consequences for social behaviour. The weakening of organized labour, the destruction of long-standing skills and crafts, the influence of the European Community on corporate business and industrial culture have all created tension and uncertainty. The family unit itself has become weaker and its influence in transmitting values correspondingly less strong. Indeed, in some areas it is reaching the point where the school seems willy-nilly to be saddled with the task of making up the deficiencies left by the home. We have witnessed the emergence of the teenager as a separate class with its own tastes and values, courted by advertisers, flattered by media attention, saturated in its own music, with money to spend and a corresponding sense of liberation.

We are warned by the National Economic Development Office to expect that, during this decade, as much as 80 per cent or even 90 per cent of any increase in the labour force will come from women with children. Industry will need to be flexible and inventive to accommodate such a change and so will our schools. Society will continue in a state of transition and will throw a heavy responsibility upon educationalists to examine afresh their methods. Is it surprising that teaching has become more stressful and can it be reasonable to expect teachers to carry this without more help?

The reach of education is not wide enough to embrace the needs of our changing society. Three areas in particular will have to be given a much higher priority—the provision of many more nursery schools; more and better education and training for the 16- to 19-year-olds; and the creation of a broad system of re-education and re-training for those in adult life of all ages.

There have been numerous educational changes in the 1980s but there has been no overall study of the fundamental purposes of education until the recently announced National Commission on Education set up with Lord Walton as Chairman. This has been established precisely for the purpose of defining Britain's educational goals and defining practical means to meet them. The Commission starts off with a favourable wind. Public concern is at a high level, the political parties are giving their educational policies a high profile, there is more agreement among educationalists than might seem on the surface, and parents are alert to the need for improvement. Walton could turn out to be as important as Robbins was in shaping the future.

Every study must start from the needs of the individual child. Whatever their background, their disability or their home, the responsibility and the trust of society is to offer to every one of our children the best education we can provide. During my own childhood, as long ago as the 1920s, many were denied the education they were capable of and this undoubtedly hardened my own convictions, which are best summed up in the words of R. H. Tawney: 'What a wise parent would wish for their children, so the State must wish for all its children.' To me, conscious of my own educational gaps, education has always been a treasure—not to be hoarded but to be spread widely and generously. Like others of my generation I shall always be grateful to the public libraries that opened their doors to us, and to the adult educational institutions like Birkbeck, the WEA and the NCLC, which provided disciplined courses of study.

I still have some lingering regrets that, when I resigned as Chancellor of the Exchequer in 1964, the Prime Minister, Harold Wilson, did not meet my request to become instead the Secretary of State for Education. However, I have tried to repay some of my debt by becoming, for a short winter, a voluntary WEA lecturer, and, much more recently, enjoying the honour of being President of this College.

For everyone concerned about education the task remains unchanged. To increase equality of opportunity, to end underachievement, to obliterate distinctions based on a false sense of status, to ensure that we have the highest quality teachers and, above all, to endow our children with understanding. Let there be no mistake. At the end of the day, the development and the quality of our democratic society will be determined by what society does in educating its people. That is the importance of our discussions here today.

NOTES

1.   Moser, C. (1990) *Our Need for an Informed Society*, Presidential Address, British Association, London.
2.   Cassels, J. (1990) *Britain's Real Skills Shortage*. London: Policy Studies Institute.
3.   DES/WO (1991) *Education and Training for the 21st Century*, London: HMSO.
4.   Finegold, D., Keep, E., Miliband, D., Raffe, D., Spours, K. and Young, M. (1990) *A British Baccalaureat*. London: Institute for Public Policy Research.

Chapter 3

The Education Debate II
The Rt Hon. John MacGregor, OBE, MP

I am delighted to have this chance to return to the educational world, to have the opportunity to look back at Lord Callaghan's Ruskin College speech of 1976, to review progress since that time, to look at what has changed and to look toward the future.

I do not know whether Lord Callaghan made that speech because he wanted to focus on the public concern about education and educational standards which was bubbling up then, or, more mundanely, because he was laying the foundation stone for a further extension of Ruskin College. I only cheekily suggest the latter, because practising politicians know that sometimes you have something you desperately want to say and look for an opportunity to say it and sometimes you have an engagement to fulfil and desperately look for something to say. Whatever it was, and I am quite certain it was the former, it triggered what was then known as the Great Debate. The speech touched a very sensitive spot at the time. It touched, particularly, sensitivities among what might be described as the ultimate consumers of education, the parents, industrialists and so on, and this is reflected in his speech. It really has been fascinating, therefore, to look back at the speech and be reminded of its actual content. I picked out several issues which it raised and I would like to analyse progress on these and to indicate where I agree or I disagree with the implications behind Lord Callaghan's then remarks and indeed some of what he has said in the anniversary speech. I say implications, because, as Lord Callaghan has said, much of the speech was framed in terms of questions and raising issues rather than providing specific answers. It may come as a surprise that there will be a lot more agreement than disagreement. But equally I shall be claiming more credit for this Government's performance in achieving results than his own. I would also like to highlight some areas which his speech did not touch on—and that's not a criticism, because I am sure there are going to be lots of areas that my speech does not touch on—but which I do regard as very important.

First, I would like to associate myself entirely with him on this basic point. As Celts we both give the highest priority to giving our children the best possible education to develop their talents to the full. Not only for itself and because it opens up for the individual huge interests in life which remain with him or her thereafter, but also because it provides equality of opportunity for all those who take advantage of it. But as practical men, I think we both go further. I believe that just as important—indeed, today, I would say even more important—is the need to ensure that our young people have the broad range of skills, and at an increasingly intense level, to enable them to acquire and to keep jobs and to adjust constantly in this increasingly competitive world. I know that puts the functional rather than philosophical aspects of education first, but for me it is now so very important. Lord Callaghan in his Ruskin speech put it this way, 'There is no virtue in producing socially well-adjusted members of society who are unemployed because they do not have the skills.'

I sometimes found myself in hot water when I was Secretary of State for Education in some educational meetings for putting such a heavy focus on this functional aspect of education, but I make no apology for it. If you look at what is happening in Japan, Germany, the United States and, perhaps above all, the new challenging economies of the Asian Pacific region, there can be no doubt that we shall neither sustain our standards of living nor create the resources to produce an expanding education system, let alone other public services, unless the education system delivers the skills that our economy and our people will require. And the Ruskin speech contained many passages of concern that education was not delivering what industry and commerce were seeking.

I set alongside the Ruskin speech the following quote:

> We are bound to add that our evidence appears to show that our industrial classes have not even that basis of a sound general education on which alone a technical education can rest. In fact our deficiency is not merely a deficiency in technological education, but in general intelligence and, unless we remedy this want, we shall gradually but surely find that our undeniable superiority in wealth and perhaps in energy shall not save us from decline.

That was from the Schools Enquiry Royal Commission of 1868[1] at a time when we thought that we had the educational, technological and industrial leads. When I was asked by the *Times Educational Supplement* shortly after my appointment as Secretary of State to do a short piece for them, for a Christmas edition, on the three books I would pick out from my reading in the year just past, I think I caused some flutters in some circles by including Correlli Barnett's *The Audit of War*,[2] which I re-read immediately on my appointment as Secretary of State. The reason for this was that I wanted to remind myself of what I remembered as a devastating critique of the state of preparedness of British industry and commerce as we embarked on the Second World War, particularly in comparison with Germany. On page after page it underlined the unjustified complacency that ran through so many strands of our national life and attributed much of it to the educational system of the previous many decades.

Another book which had a similar influence upon me in the 1980s was Martin Wiener's *English Culture and the Decline of the Industrial Spirit 1850–1980*.[3] And so I associate myself wholly with the concluding remarks of Lord Callaghan's speech today when he was talking about the task for education, to increase equality of opportunity and to end under-achievement. I so much agree with that, because I have seen still in too many of our schools under-achievement by pupils, although I think it is much, much less of a problem than it was some years ago. To obliterate distinctions based on a false sense of status, to ensure that we have the highest quality teachers, and above all to endow our children with understanding, I absolutely associate myself with that.

This leads me to the first theme I want to pick up from the original Ruskin speech—'the need to improve relations between industry and education'. Lord Callaghan has already indicated what he was referring to then, the concerns among many in industry that the schools were not providing the skills that industry—and I think by that we mean all employers—required; that there was insufficient co-ordination between schools and employers; that there were too many vacancies in science and engineering places in universities and polytechnics; and that there was no desire among too many school leavers to join industry.

I do believe that there has been a sea change in the 1980s in this respect. This is the first theme I want to take up. We may still have quite a long way to go, but there has been a substantial change in attitudes on all sides. I remember one of my first jobs in government was as Parliamentary Under Secretary at the Department of Industry, where I was Minister for Small Businesses, and at that time I also had responsibility for the Industry Education Unit in the Department of Industry. It was a tiny unit, very small indeed, but I spent a lot of time going round the country on that activity. Although there were a lot of good things going on, I have to say that there were great divisions of attitude and a lack of co-operation between what was then sadly regarded as the two sides. There were schools which did not have strong co-operation with local employers and did not see that as their role and far too many employers who simply criticized the schools and never did anything to help. I believe, and this is one of the things that delighted me when I went to the DES, that we have really changed that very considerably indeed. We can see that most big companies today—I would say nearly all the big companies—actually now give high priority to getting closer to schools, to being involved in one form or another with education. We have seen it in the growth of Compacts, very important not only in this industry–education link, but also I think in improving education in the inner-city areas to which Lord Callaghan referred. There are now over fifty Compacts and they are all in inner-city areas. I found companies took those very seriously indeed. We see it in local education–business partnerships; we see it in the Training and Enterprise Councils. But above all we see it simply in initiatives by industry and responses, or very often, initiatives from schools. Indeed one of the things that struck me was that often it was the schools who were taking the initiative at the local level in the first place and I wholly welcome that. Partly because of my view of the Martin Wiener problem and partly because of my anxiety to see the British economy developing in the way that I think it now is and certainly ought to in terms of enterprise and efficiency, recreating the enterprise spirit, I was very anxious to have a proper understanding taking place in schools of the processes of wealth creation. I have therefore welcomed all the young enterprise initiatives and so on. We still have some considerable way to go in encouraging enough employers to encourage key managers and others of their employees to play a full part as school governors and I know how many headteachers and teachers would welcome a greater participation there. Big companies like IBM and BP and Shell have been engaging in programmes with teachers from primary and secondary schools, sometimes doing joint training courses between some of their senior employees and headteachers. What has struck me is how often, when you talk to the companies, what they say is how impressed they are with the quality of the headteachers and the teachers who have participated in the programme. That is doing quite a bit to help to improve the teacher status question with which we are all concerned.

But I believe that, having seen a sea change in the 1980s, we still have a long way to go. There are some areas I would pick out which I think are challenges for the 1990s which Lord Callaghan referred to then and today and where I would like to see much more progress. One has to be in science and engineering where it is disappointing to see that the percentage of students on science-related courses in universities is the same today as it was in 1980, at some 40 per cent. It is interesting that in the polytechnics and higher education colleges that figure has improved quite markedly during the 1980s, with the figure for them up from 26 per cent in 1980 to 33 per cent today. I also would very much wish to see more girls involved in science and in engineering, an area where there is still much to be done.

Theme two is, of course, resources. In his Ruskin speech Lord Callaghan referred to the massive injection of resources into education, though he added this interesting rider,

> In present circumstances there can be little expectation of further increased resources being made
> available at any rate for the time being and I fear that those whose only answer to these problems is
> to call for more money will be disappointed.

Shades, I think, of the IMF intervention as the Ruskin College speech was delivered in October 1976! There has been a massive injection of further resources since then. At that time the current spending was £6 billion on education and to-day it is £26 billion. When people argue that simply more resources is the answer to our education problems they should reflect on the fact that we spend a higher percentage of our Gross National Product on public education than Germany, the United States and Japan.

Recently I have been in the United States, Germany and New Zealand, in particular, on educational visits and what was striking in the United States was the degree of concern about the standards of school education. I went to the National Science Foundation in Washington to discuss scientific research and spent the entire day hearing from them how worried they were about the levels of science and mathematics education in schools in the United States. In Germany I was much struck by the fact that, although I believe they are way ahead of us in the 16–19 age group, to which I wish to return, as far as university education is concerned they were looking to much that was going on here because of some concerns of what was happening in their higher education. In New Zealand, certainly, they are going through major changes in education similar to changes introduced in England and Wales.

So it is not just a question of resources and I have to agree with Lord Callaghan that there will always be limits. That means that if we simply talk about resources we are doing less than justice to the Education Debate. At one level we need to devote more and more attention to ensuring that the money is wisely spent. Hence one reason for my enthusiasm for local management of schools (LMS). I do believe that decisions are taken more quickly and more effectively, that local priorities are established properly and maintenance work, for example, is done more cheaply through local management of schools. Therefore I believe that it is a change which will be permanent in the 1990s, which will enable us to spend money more effectively. I also believe that it is important to ensure that as much as possible of the money which LEAs control does get down into the schools and that is why I strongly supported the initiative to achieve this when I was Secretary of State and support what has been done since.

At another level we need to ensure that resources are directed at the right priorities. Deciding the allocation of priorities is one of the biggest and most difficult issues in government and in politics. I am sure Lord Callaghan, with his great experience, will agree with me. It raises questions like the degree to which priority is given to nursery education—though, in fact, now something like 78 per cent of all 4-year-olds are in one form or another of nursery education—versus the big post-16 challenge. How much goes into science and how to achieve it? It also raises the issues that we have been grappling with in what Lord Callaghan described as the market-oriented policies, but which I think are actually about something else.

In the context of resources I wish to comment on student loans. I took that controversial bill through the House of Commons. What struck me most, as we embarked on the process was, first, the scale of increasing numbers going into higher education in the 1990s. It would be very difficult to have funded that entirely through public funding and to have carried on the same level of student maintenance support. The second thing was that we were way ahead of any other country in the degree of public funding for student maintenance that we gave. So I actually believe that the student loan decision was also about allocation of funding priorities.

This leads me on to my third theme. Lord Callaghan in his Ruskin speech voiced considerable doubts about standards. Indeed, this was the issue that was most picked up in the debate thereafter. He expressed a personal view that he was inclined to think that there should be a basic curriculum with universal standards. Well now we have got it! We have, twelve years later, a National Curriculum approved by Parliament. The basic debate I believe about whether we should or should not have a National Curriculum is over, but, as he quite rightly said today, the issues affecting its implementation will be with us for some years. I was proud to be involved in those early stages of making the National Curriculum work. I agree there is a problem about speed. Lord Callaghan referred to 'innovation fatigue' and it is important to get the balance right. However the National Curriculum will not be fully in place until 1996/7. If we agree that placing greater emphasis on science, technology, modern languages and a number of subjects that are now firmly in the National Curriculum for all are so important then we agree that we cannot afford to wait. I can understand the feelings of so many in the teaching profession, particularly, of course, those at the primary school level who were dealing with Key Stage 1, which, I always explain to general audiences, is jargon for age 7, who felt over-burdened and overwhelmed.

On the other hand, increasingly as they got to grips with the changes, they discovered that what was being talked about, by and large, was best practice and I believe we have now got over that worry about speed. I hope it is recognized that we are trying to phase the National Curriculum in at a pace with which the schools can cope. It is a question of balance because, if we are concerned about not enough of our young people acquiring skills, then we have got to get on with it fairly quickly. I did respond very sympathetically to the feeling of overburdening from many teachers about the National Curriculum. What was happening was that so many with very strong views about what they would like to see in the educational system used the Education Reform Act as a way of having them injected into the system. Further, they were trying in one form or another to advise schools. In the early stages I had a great deal of sympathy with those teachers who just pointed to the amount of paper that every week was crossing their desks from a whole variety of sources. We have certainly tried to address that. There will be difficulties and there will have to be changes and I certainly felt, and I notice that my successor has felt equally, that the original SEAC pilot studies on Standard Assessment Tasks (SATs) and then the subsequent work, which I tried to cut down quite a bit, were oppressive, overburdensome and excessive.

I think one of the problems here is the job which very often does fall in the end to Ministers who are changing posts from time to time, to get the balance between the statutory educational advisory bodies who are trying to reach an ideal as they see it and what practically can be done in the schools. I have no doubts that it was sensible to have a pilot study on SATs and sensible that we go on being prepared to revise and change in response to practical experience.

One of the issues which was very much with us in the early stages of the National Curriculum was getting the quart into a pint pot in the post-14 stage of the National Curriculum. I agree very much with Lord Callaghan that the National Curriculum must not be made, as he said, into a straitjacket. I think there was a danger of this in the post-14 Key Stage 4. We were not giving enough flexibility to the schools particularly at that stage, but something had to give and that something was not to give quite the same priority to art and music as we were giving to the other subjects. This will continue to be an issue where we must be prepared to adjust.

With regard to the advisory bodies and all those who are involved in the National Curriculum it is important to have not just people who are from the educational establishment and educational experts, but to have people from outside as well, very much involved in the development of the National Curriculum. However, I fully recognize, and I hope that it was clear in everything I was trying to do, that we must carry the profession with us.

On teaching methods I certainly share what I detected were very strongly Lord Callaghan's reservations in 1976 about the danger of child-centred learning going too far and I think that also applies to putting too much emphasis on coursework in the examination system. I think he is right to say that we have to achieve a balance. I also want to turn, briefly and very tentatively, to the argument about A-Levels, Higginson, and post-16 education. I am unrepentant in saying that there is much good in A-Levels and what we do not want to lose is the academic rigour, the depth and excellence of A-Levels. On the other hand, and particularly as a Scot, I recognize the importance of not specializing too early. I have always been grateful in my life for the fact that I did not and therefore I am receptive to the idea that we should provide a broader spread in the sixth form. There are some very interesting ideas coming out as to how this might be achieved, but I have to say that I am not one of those who would wish to ditch A-Levels. We are now seeing increasing numbers going on into sixth forms. Many more youngsters want to stay on in school after 16, not least because of the impact of GCSE, but this means that there are increasing numbers for whom the A-Level route, the wholly academic route, is inappropriate. I do, therefore, share the views of those who argue for modular courses, for more opportunities to transfer and so on.

The fourth area to which I wish to turn, which was classified by Lord Callaghan as a field needing study, is the proper way of monitoring the use of resources in order to maintain a national standard of performance. This is a huge subject in itself, but much has happened in recent years and I believe much has been put in place to enable better monitoring in the 1990s. One obvious measurement is the number of people staying on at school. That is a clear measurement of the increasing success of the educational system and although I agree that we have quite a way to go to reach the standards of some countries, I think we ought to recognize just how much has been achieved in recent years: 41 per cent were staying on at the age of sixteen in 1979/80, 60 per cent today, and, if you add training into that, something like over 90 per cent of all our youngsters in the age 16–18 age group are receiving either full-time education or training. The problem, as I think we all recognize, still comes at the 17- and 18-year-old level where, although there has been a considerable improvement, it is not good enough. But I believe that we are seeing a revolution taking place at this very moment. It is also reflected in the number of candidates getting good grades, for example, in GCSE—up from 23 per cent in 1975/76 to 35 per cent today—and above all by the number going into higher and further education. The mechanisms now being evolved are designed to enable us to track improvements of standards through the school system as well. For example, the SATs themselves, the reporting to parents of children's achievement, the reporting of schools overall so that standards can be tracked nationally, school reports, records of achievements and funding per pupil, which I think has in it a mechanism for improving standards of performance and even teacher assessment. So there is much that has been going on that I think will help us in that regard.

The final area of study that Lord Callaghan identified was the inspectorate in relation to national standards. HMI are very widely respected in the educational system, are dedicated professionals and have done a great deal of useful work. I had two concerns when I was Secretary of State. One, which was not really to do with the HMIs themselves at all I have to say, was the way in which the media covered a lot of their reports, much of it unbalanced. The reports were trying to indicate how much progress had been achieved in given areas, but quite rightly always point to areas where further improvement is necessary. So often, however, what was plucked out in the media comment was what was regarded as a devastating indictment of schools' or teachers' performance. The 80 per cent 'excellent' or 'good' or 'satisfactory' was ignored, and the 20 per cent 'could do better' or 'poor' was highlighted. This not only gave a false impression of progress, it had something to do also with the demoralizing effect upon good teachers. I remember in particular one report which came out and on the day was put across as a slamming of schools' performance in some of the popular press. I was going round schools in Cheshire and Staffordshire and was getting a very fed-up and upset response from the teachers that day. I had to tell them what I knew was in the rest of that report. The worry is that that kind of unbalanced reporting can actually affect parents' perceptions too.

Second, and more important, I was sometimes left with the impression in reading the reports, that like management consultants, inspectors gave their general observations, but, unlike management consultants, did not sufficiently focus on precise action programmes. Sometimes, not always by any means, my feeling after reading a report was 'Yes, but now what do we do?' I am interested to discover that in New Zealand they are in the process of a radical re-casting of their inspectorate. I very much hope the reforms which my successor is now undertaking will lead to a more open system and in particular that the requirement on governors to produce an action programme will make it sharper-edged.

Now I wish to turn briefly to some of the issues which Lord Callaghan has mentioned today, but which were not included in his Ruskin speech. First, the teaching profession, status and rewards. I still have reservations about a General Teaching Council, relating to its functions and responsibilities. I have seen a variety of suggestions and they do not always equate with those of the General Medical Council or the Bar Council. While I have some reservations about that, I very strongly agree with him about the importance of constantly raising the status of teachers as a profession. I am going to be controversial now, quite deliberately, because I felt very strongly about it at the time. I think the teaching profession was let down by some of the ways in which teachers' apparent views were put across by their leaders in the early 1980s. I know how easy it is to have the media focus, television in particular, only on the people who are prepared to say fairly strident—I am trying to avoid the word outrageous—things, but I do not think that helped the status of the profession. What I was trying to do, what I believe is so important, is to talk constantly about the many good teachers we have. It is surprising when you do the excellent response you get from audiences that are not in the educational world. It is necessary to talk also about the importance of the teaching profession having a constructive attitude to the new governing bodies, because that is undoubtedly the way to obtain a great deal of local and public involvement and to improve the salary structure. One of the key things that the Interim Advisory Committee was able to achieve was to improve the salary structure itself, and I strongly welcome the new Review Body.

Second, and here I come to an area where I would like to explain my difference of view with Lord Callaghan, the whole question of the greater involvement if you like of the consumer— parents and employers. We are seeing it in the Parent's Charter, we are seeing it in the much greater responsibility given to governing bodies, we are seeing it in the open choice for parents, we are seeing it in the LMS formula funding and we are seeing it in a number of other ways. This is not a question of having the competitive element, as it were, in the market-place for consumer goods. I think what this is all about is those who benefit from the educational process being engaged in the process itself and above all enabling them to exercise their choices by their decisions as much as possible as to where they want to send their children. Now I agree that there are many areas where this will not apply, market towns in well-scattered rural communities, for example, sometimes in inner city areas, but it is a process which will improve standards at the same time.

Let me also turn to a controversial area, City Technology Colleges. I was keen on them because I believe in not having a single uniform system. I believe in having experiment, a degree of variety of opportunities for choice. I was also of course anxious to see improvements in technology and it is another way of getting a greater involvement of business. They are all focused on inner city areas. In going to visit CTCs I was much struck by the effect that they had on the parents in those areas. Now there is no doubt that the schools are popular; they are attracting large numbers of parents and they are one way of helping to improve the inner city areas. I therefore do not think that the motivation for all of these things is simply to inject the market economy; it is to achieve a greater opportunity for choice, greater involvement and also to improve standards.

Let me turn next to parity of esteem, because I feel that this is the next major area of reform. We have made quite a lot of progress through the 1980s. We have seen the BTEC and CNAA reforms and I think the Further Education White Paper will take us a good deal further. I do not want to get into too much of the area of training, but I think that the pilot that we have been doing on training credits gives us a very interesting way through that problem of trying to motivate the youngster who still leaves school at 16 without any educational aspirations and then suddenly discovers that, if he is going to be able to hold down a decent job, he has got to get more training. By giving the training credit I think you provide a motivation in a form that young people most recognize. I very much agree with the thought that what is most of all required here is a cultural shift of attitude. I agree that the difficulty about the A-Levels is that they have always been recognized as the route to academic excellence and those who fail their A-Levels have been regarded as failures. That is an attitude of mind we must eradicate, but the positive side of it, the one that is still going to require quite a cultural change, is to get the community as a whole, parents and pupils, to recognize that achieving technical qualifications is every bit as important and every bit as desirable. When I went to Germany and studied what they were doing there, some of the mechanisms that we are employing now are as good as theirs. The fundamental difference was that every German parent regarded it as a mark of achievement that their child got that qualification. It is deep-seated and it has not been deep-seated enough in parts of our country.

Finally, recognizing that you cannot cover everything in one speech, I come to what I regard as the one big omission of the Ruskin speech, and in what Lord Callaghan has said today. This is the higher education sector. We are seeing a real cultural shift in attitude in this country which I greatly welcome. Lord Callaghan's figure of 15 per cent going into higher education is quite a bit out of date. The age participation index in 1976 was 13.3 per cent. It only moved up very marginally throughout the early 1980s. By 1987 it was 14.6 per cent—that is where I think the 15 per cent figure comes from—but, as all of us who have been involved since then know, every year our expectations based on demographic trends and based on previous experience have been wildly out. We have always under-estimated the new numbers that are going into higher education in the next year and the figure for 1992 of age participation is likely to be about 25 per cent. It is certainly only just below that in 1991. There has been an increase of 10 per cent a year in the numbers going into universities and polytechnics in the last few years. I believe that this is partly because the education reforms and the Great Education Debate which Lord Callaghan started have created much more interest in education in this country than we had earlier, so there is the cultural shift taking place. It is also because there is increasingly a recognition, as Lord Callaghan said, that, if you are going to hold down worthwhile jobs in the years ahead, you simply have got to have a broad base of educational skills and particular skills on top of that. I also hope and believe it is because of some of the education reforms. Robbins did produce the first great expansion of the educational system in recent decades, but it was not a system that was wholly geared to responding to needs out there. I think that what we have seen in the freeing of the polytechnics from local education authorities, what we have seen in the greater emphasis on funding at the higher education level depending on the numbers being attracted in, is creating a much more aggressive and outward-looking attitude by our higher education institutions and I greatly welcome this. I think it is important to be innovating, it is important to be seeing what the market-place wants, it is important to be looking ahead, as you have done so successfully here in Swansea in the courses you have developed linking engineering and modern languages. That is where a lot of the demand is going to come and one of the things that most pleased me when I was Secretary of State for Education was to discover that the United Kingdom was the main beneficiary, or one of the three main beneficiaries who were all about the same, of the ERASMUS programme. And why? Because our higher education institutions now are very innovative, aggressive and are looking for the opportunities to go on building up the new courses and building up the new relationships. Therefore I think that we are in the process of a very exciting change in higher education which the figures are already showing. If you look at the effectiveness of our higher education system, in other words the very low wastage rates we have of those who come into our institutions and therefore the very high percentages that qualify, and make the comparison with the Americans or the Germans (though not the Japanese) and add the two together, this very big increase in recent years, coupled with our great effectiveness, puts us on a par already with the countries to which we are looking for our targets.

I have indicated a number of areas in which I hope we will continue to advance. I believe that there has been a great deal of progress in recent years and I think it is coming out in the very encouraging way in which our higher education is now developing. It has been a great pleasure for me to share a few of these thoughts with you. I hope it has indicated that I continue to have the closest possible interest in education. I was especially delighted to come here to Swansea because it was Lord Callaghan who really set the focus again on the Great Debate.

NOTES

1.   Schools Inquiry Commission (1868) *The Taunton Commission*. London: HMSO.
2.   Barnett, C. (1986) *The Audit of War: The Illusion and Reality of Britain as a Great Nation*. London: Macmillan.
3.   Wiener, M.J. (1981) *English Culture and the Decline of the Industrial Spirit, 1850-1980*. Cambridge: Cambridge University Press.

Chapter 4

Looking to the Future

Ted Wragg

I am particularly glad to be sharing this platform with Lord Callaghan and John MacGregor. It must have been around about the tenth anniversary, maybe a bit after, of the Ruskin College speech, that I did a half-hour Radio Four interview with Lord Callaghan, asking him about what was in his mind when he gave his speech and what he thought about what had happened since. It was, I thought, a good programme. When you do a Radio Four programme you usually get a hundred letters all written in spidery green biro, but there was some very positive feedback from non-spidery green biro writers on this one, and particularly, it should be said, from the studio manager. When Lord Callaghan had gone home I said to the studio manager, 'What did you make of that?' and he replied how much he had enjoyed it. But then he said, 'It's so nice to hear that kind of politician's talk, because often politicians don't talk like that nowadays.' Lord Callaghan had talked about his own childhood and how he had been driven to try and do things for people because of his own experiences.

I have not had a great deal of time for certain recent Secretaries of State, but I did for John MacGregor and I say that, not because he happens to be here, but because it was true. I thought he was the one Secretary of State we have had recently who did try to manage the system and to listen to people. As a result of my views on that, when I was profiled in *The Independent*, with one of those cartoons that is drawn from real photographs, they interviewed somebody from the right wing—whether it was from the rotating eye balls faction or not I am not sure—but this person said, 'Well, of course, he thinks very highly of John MacGregor, he's just the sort of chap who would'.

What I intend to do in this address is to go into the future and into the past and into the present, but I am going to start in the past and then go into the future and then come back to the present, which may seem a bizarre way of doing it, but I hope it has a logic to it. I want to go into the past, because around the time that Lord Callaghan launched the Great Debate, there was another version of the Great Debate that went on in the House of Commons through a Parliamentary Select Committee, to which I was specialist adviser. Beforehand I did not really know too much about how these things worked and I gained a lot of respect for the MPs of all parties who served on that committee, because some of them worked very hard indeed. There were very conscientious people like Janet Fookes and Sir Anthony Meyer from the Conservative Party and Brian Davies and Peter Harvey from the Labour Party. They came regularly to all the sessions and we were able to take evidence from a variety of people. It was very interesting, as the debate was going on around the country, to have people coming from bodies like the CBI, the TUC, and the Exam Boards. Ministers came along, people from the teacher unions, individuals came too, and we were able to collect an enormous amount of information not only about the present, as it was back in 1976/77, but speculations about the future. It is interesting now to see which of those came true and which did not.

I was particularly impressed by some of the evidence from people like employers and trades union representatives, from a very mixed kind of educational background. We have heard from Lord Callaghan how some things that were not going too well at that time may be better now. The whole business of school/industry links is a good example. At that time the careers advice in schools was absolutely appalling. We had evidence from both the careers service in local authorities and from careers advisory teachers in schools and many schools at that time just had a room, if that, with a few pamphlets. What we have seen in the 1980s is a lot of schools working very hard to establish relationships with employers, not only through schemes like the Technical and Vocational Education Initiative, but also through other initiatives as well and that has been a positive development. Now many of those people from industry are serving on school governing bodies as well, so I see that as a plus.

There was a concern at that time, which has not gone away, about the achievement of children who were in the lowest achieving sector and it is to Lord Joseph's credit that it was one of the matters that he raised as a Secretary of State and showed an interest in. There was at that time a pamphlet called *The Unqualified, Untrained and Unemployed*.[1] It was about the bottom 15 per cent of the achievement range. I look now at the many comparisons that are made with Germany, which I visit quite often; in fact, I was teaching in German schools in June this year. I do not think they have an edge on us in primary education; indeed I do not think they have an edge on us in a number of other areas. But where I think they do outscore us very heavily is in vocational education, which is excellent in Germany, and also in the education of lower ability children. I have seen a number of schools that do excellent work in this respect and we have a great deal to learn from them.

However, I think it should be said that over the last fifteen years or so we have gone from a situation where, in the late 1960s and early 1970s, the great majority of children left school with no qualifications at all, to a situation more recently where children, in some cases of very modest ability, are leaving school with a number of albeit low grades, but nonetheless several GCSEs. Go back to the early 1960s, and only 20 per cent of children left school with anything, usually O-Levels at that time. I do not know this year's figure, but the most recent figures show that about 90–91 per cent of children are awarded a graded GCSE. I know it is very easy to be contemptuous of the lower grades of GCSE, but I was teaching a GCSE class in German in one of the first cohorts that went through and I saw children getting lowish grades GCSE. If you had sent them to Germany and they had gone shopping, lived in a family, or whatever, they could have survived. I wish I knew as much Japanese, Arabic, Spanish and Swahili as they knew German, because then I could survive in those countries and I cannot because I do not know any of those languages. So I think we have to recognize that, even with the lower achieving children, where there has been a lot of criticism and where there is quite a deal of concern understandably, there has been some progress.

Also there was concern about the education of girls, which Lord Callaghan mentioned. It was not long after the Sex Discrimination Act, which I think had a notable influence on the education system. I will give you one example. In 1976/77 we looked at the number of boys and girls taking

A-Level Physics; in that year it was 25,000 boys and 5,000 girls. There is no good reason for a five to one split like that. It is still not fifty fifty today, but it is much nearer two and a half to one to three to one rather than five to one. There has been a distinct shift over those years. It is now no longer the case that, if there is a girl coming into a university department to do engineering, the local press rush round to film the one girl among eighty male engineers. That is no longer regarded at a curiosity, because there are more girls coming forward. There have been schemes like GIST which some of you will know about, Girls Into Science and Technology, specifically aimed at trying to get more girls to do science and technology. Back in 1976 it was a real concern and it was an enormous waste of talent. There were people who could do these subjects, but, for social reasons and social pressures that adolescents can sometimes generate for themselves and sometimes we can unwittingly signal, bright girls were not going into science and technology. It was regrettable and it is beginning to change.

In 1978/79 there were major surveys of primary[2] and secondary[3] education which those of you working in education at the time will recall. The primary schools survey, for example, said that in only one class in ten was there a decent science programme. There was very little physical science and there was very little on scientific process such as testing hypotheses and doing experiments. I think this is one of the notable achievements of the National Curriculum which I will shortly go on to be very critical of, but I would like to say first that now, in primary schools, we have much better primary science teaching. I have been teaching both 5-year-olds and 7-year-olds myself in the last two years and I know that we are doing science that would not have been done in that particular school until about three or four years ago, so that, I think, is also a step forward. The HMI secondary school survey, a survey of nearly 400 secondary schools in 1979 published in 1980, also had some critical remarks in it. Again, if you look at some of those criticisms, you can go through them one by one and you can say in certain cases things have been done by people in schools to rectify points of criticism that came out of that debate somewhere between 1976 and about 1980. So I think there has been a series of changes that have happened that have had a positive effect and I welcome them. On a wider front, the involvement of more people, including parents, in governing bodies, is greatly to be welcomed, as is making parents a more central part of the partnership. I welcome all those.

However, let me move on to say a little bit about another prediction that I made, this time in 1980. In 1980 we produced at Exeter, in our Perspectives series, a collection of papers called *The Core Curriculum*,[4] as it then was. I wrote a paper in it called 'State-approved knowledge? Ten steps down the slippery slope', which I thought was a fairly neutral-sounding title. At that time we had only one of those ten steps and now we have seven of them. I do not think it was ever Lord Callaghan's intention in generating a debate that there should be as much state intrusion into the detail of curriculum and process as there has been and when I take a look at the future I will give some of the reasons why I feel concerned about that.

Let me give you some of the steps that were in that article. We already had step one, centrally-prescribed broad aims. There were all those DES and Government papers that said that education should develop the whole child and so on, statements that only psychopaths would dissent from. They were innocuous broad generalities, things of which we would all approve. But then, if you go down to the next step, centrally-prescribed subjects, we now have them. Number three was centrally-prescribed amounts of time, which we have not quite got, but there have been arguments about whether science should be 10 per cent or 20 per cent of the week or should it, in the end, be 12½ per cent of the week. This is not laid down in the Statutes, but there is a sort of understanding about how much of the week is going to be prescribed centrally.

I went on to speculate about further steps like specific objectives. At that time I quoted

American examples of school district programmes that said children should learn to, say, multiply two two-digit numbers at a certain age. We did not have those, but we have them now. They are the statements in the attainment targets. Some of them are very prescriptive and some are more loosely framed, so that they are capable of imaginative interpretations and I welcome that looser phrasing sometimes. Next came centrally-prescribed textbooks. We do not have them. There are countries, of course, which have a National Curriculum with centrally-prescribed textbooks. The nearest we have is the prescription of the *Little Twinky* series for the testing of children at 7, where you have that list of set books that you have to do the tests from and you have to choose a hundred words. I gather one of them is ninety-seven words long so presumably you have to read out 'Copyright reserved Toronto', but we do not yet have a centrally prescribed set of books. There is free choice and we have a very wide choice in this country; a hundred and fifty or more published reading schemes for example gives enormous choice and, if you go to the National Textbook Library in London, you can see a vast choice on almost any topic you can think of. I sometimes go in there and expect maybe there will be relatively little in, say, remedial mathematics teaching, but there are shelves full, even of readers for teaching children Russian. So there is a lot of choice, but not prescribed yet.

Centrally-prescribed teaching strategies was the next step. Well we do not have those yet, but we are beginning to go down that line and I hope we do not go too far. Again there are countries where the teaching strategies are prescribed. There are countries which say if you are teaching a foreign language you must teach that foreign language in the language concerned. We have not done that, though we have said, if you teach a foreign language, maybe it would be a good idea to use the language as much as possible. But it is not a requirement that lessons should be entirely in the foreign language.

On the other hand, we are beginning to see, for me, too much intrusion into teaching methods. For example, it was said that there would be money available for language and reading-type schemes in inner city areas, provided that these were according to traditional methods. That always alarms me when I see it, because I have some books in my room written by the Reverend Brewer in 1870. The children actually chant out slogans. The teacher would ask, 'Who was Henry the Eighth?' and the children had to reply 'The Son of Henry the Seventh'. The next question is, 'How was he?' and they have to say 'Bluff, handsome and right royal'. Then, in the Reverend Brewer's Geography book, the question is 'What is the climate of England?' and the answer is 'Moist, but healthy' and 'What is the character of the British people?', 'Brave, but very persevering'. I am all for that, but I think we have to be careful if the Government is going to start prescribing, albeit obliquely in this case, teaching methods.

I have been rung up by journalists writing articles on the teaching of reading, asking, 'Are you for phonics or real books?' I would say, 'Yes, definitely'. It was a ludicrous debate and it was interesting when HMI came out with their report and said only 3 per cent of teachers were exclusively phonics and only 5 per cent were exclusively real books and the vast majority actually use a mixture of methods. It seems to me to have been one of the healthy features of our system that teachers have used their professionalism to choose methods that they judge to be right for an individual child, for a particular group or for a whole class. I hope that we preserve that.

The later steps in the article were government-prescribed tests, which we now have. Next, that test scores would be put into league tables, which is coming. Then, centrally-prescribed remedial programmes, which we do not have. The last one was teachers being dismissed if they do not teach the central prescriptions. We do have that since it is a legal requirement to teach the National Curriculum and, although nobody has been sacked yet, my guess is that somebody will one day be sacked for not teaching the National Curriculum, probably as an excuse for some other misdemeanour. It will not be done in its own right, because frankly you would be sacking 450,000 teachers at this very moment if you did that. A teacher was dismissed in Hertfordshire, for example, for not teaching the agreed syllabus in R.E.

I want to look at the future now, because I want to pick up some of the points Lord Callaghan made. Alvin Toffler[5] said 'All education is a vision of the future and if you don't have a vision of the future you're betraying the nation's youth' and I think that is a very powerful statement about one of the central purposes of education, that we need to have a vision of the future so we have to look ahead to the twenty-first century and we have to predict what kind of life people will lead. We have heard some hints already about the kind of life people will lead because we can make intelligent guesses on the base of what is happening now. Back in 1976 we were in the middle of a decade in which one million jobs disappeared from manufacturing industry and we thought that was bad enough at the time, but in the first five years of the 1980s another one and a half million jobs disappeared from manufacturing industry. In the city where I was born, Sheffield, twenty-five thousand jobs went from steel in two years. You may well say well what is the difference between that and the industrial revolutions that happened in the nineteenth century. There is a big difference. The first is we can now see where those industrial revolutions went to. There used to be over 30 per cent of the people working on the land in the nineteenth century; this year it is about 2 per cent. So we can see that people left the land and went into the factories, but during the 1970s and 1980s, when people left the factories it was very difficult to see what they were going to go into.

One prediction was of an enormous boom in recreation and leisure, resulting in lots of jobs there, except that in order to fund recreation and leisure you have to be as prosperous as possible and, if times are hard, then it is often recreation and leisure that takes a knock either at a personal level or for a local authority, or a school. That is what tends to get shaded at the edges and so we have not quite had the recreation and leisure boom, although it is a growing industry. One prediction, for example, that has been around for some time, is that in the twenty-first century, certainly in the early years, recreation, leisure and education itself will be amongst the major employers and that may well still come true. If it did come true that would have considerable implications for life in school. Even if it has not come yet, it may well come more in the next century, but, if you are going to have more 'non-work' time, it is very difficult to define. I was once a member of a Sports Council and Social Science Research Council working party which looked at the future of recreation and leisure. We found it very difficult to define what recreation and leisure were, because for many people it actually looked like work. If some people have spare time they would run an allotment, or they would make things, or they would mend cars, or they would paint their house and very often there was a barter system where people did each other favours and it was very like work. There were some American studies showing that, when the working week is reduced, people often fill it back up again with work-type recreation. So to some extent you need the same skills and the same knowledge in your recreation and leisure as you would need in your work. If you need to be well organized and if you need to be persistent, and if you need to have certain knowledge or certain skills for work, then you can say the same kind of thing for leisure too. So it is difficult to draw the line between the two and therefore I think to some extent unified preparation for adult life is wise. We can assume that people will need a rich array of knowledge and skills and competencies of various kinds for whatever they do in our complicated adult society, but it is difficult to say with any certainty that people will work in particular jobs.

On the other hand it is possible to say certain things about this generation of children in schools today, who in some cases may still be working in the year 2030 and beyond. If they carry on working until they are 65, they may well train and re-train more frequently, maybe several times more frequently, than their parents and grandparents ever did, because what also became clear, and Lord Callaghan mentioned this, is that those jobs that disappeared were, in the main, unskilled and semi-skilled jobs. There is a premium on skill in our society. We have the paradox of high unemployment in certain areas, but also job vacancies, and the vacancies are for people to repair micro-computers and video recorders. They are not the jobs that can readily be taken by someone who used to be a miner or a steel worker without retraining. So the message for the education system is very clear. Learning is a start, but a capacity for life-long learning is absolutely crucial. If people switch off, if they say, 'learning is not for me', or 'I was no good at school', this would be a disaster. It astounds me when I meet adults whom I regard as very bright people that when I talk to them and I say 'Well, why don't you do whatever it is?', they reply 'Count me out, I was no good at school, I'm useless'. They carry with them this stigma that they were no good. I think we have to make sure that, even if children do not perform brilliantly compared with their fellows, at least they preserve the excitement of learning, the incentive to learn, the feeling that some people take a bit longer and maybe later on in life, if they have another go, it often is the case that second time round people learn better. Sometimes then maybe they see the purpose of learning, they are actually listening. All kinds of factors are at work here. When I talk about the greater complexity of jobs for example, I do not mean only the highest level of jobs. Let me start with the highest level of jobs. Surgeons have to learn transplant techniques, triple by-pass surgery, an enormous range of new techniques, key-hole surgery and so on, but what are they are going to have to learn in the year 2000 and the year 2010? This rapid change will not stop. There are many high-grade professions where there is no moratorium on change. The changes go on, in fact they escalate, so much so that people have to become more and more specialized. But the same could be said for jobs at a more modest level. A good example is shop stewards, who used to do oral negotiation on behalf of their workmates and who now do relatively little of that, because it is mainly done in many industries at national level by national officers of unions and national representatives of employers. What they do have to do is advise their workmates about matters such as health and safety at work, or unfair dismissals. If they are going to do that, then they have to be able to read the literature that their union sends them that explains people's rights and obligations and entitlements, because if they cannot do that, they are letting their workmates down. So they still need oral competence, but they also need writing and reading competence of a kind that they have not needed before. There are many examples, alongside those jobs that were de-skilled, of jobs where the skills have become more complex and the pressures on people have become greater and I am not just talking about the world of work.

A former colleague of mine, Colin Harrison at Nottingham University, did an analysis of the reading competence that you need in adult life. Think about your daily reading. What do you have to read? Newspapers, letters, documents, things shoved through your letter-box, leaflets, quite a range of things, captions, signposts. Some are simple, some are more complex. When he did this analysis, he then graphed it according to the reading age that you need. For those not familiar with the notion, if you need a reading age of 11 for a text it means that the average 11-year-old could cope with it. He put the results on an age score line, with national newspapers on one side and documents on the other. This is what he found for national newspapers. Reading age 12: *Daily Mirror*, *The Sun*, *The Star*. I am not being contemptuous of that, by the way, because I think those are very well written newspapers, even though I do not always agree with the editorial line. 13: *Daily Mail*, 14: *The Daily Express*, 15: *Daily Telegraph*, 16: *The Guardian*, 17: *The Times*, 93: *The Scotsman*. It was not quite 93, but it was way up there!

Next he looked at the other kinds of documents that we get. Quite a lot rank alongside the sort of age score 14, 15, 16, most people should be able to manage, but when he looked at some of the key documents that we have to read, all of us, about our obligations, our entitlements and so on, some of them were quite difficult to understand. Suppose you stay in hospital, for example, and you are not happy with your stay and you want to complain. There is a leaflet, or there was when he did the analysis, called 'How to complain about your stay in hospital'. It ranked alongside *The Times*, so it would need a better reader to be able to cope with it. You may well want to complain, but the leaflet may be too difficult for you. Even harder, alongside *The Scotsman* in difficulty, was a leaflet entitled 'How to claim your free glasses'. Now there is an irony. Not only could these poor people not see, but, if they had been able to see, they would not have been able to claim their free glasses. The worst case I ever came across was with an old aunt of mine who went blind in her old age. She was sent a thing through the post which was entitled 'How to vote by proxy if you are blind'. I do not give up easily on these things. I read this about five times and I honestly had no idea what she had to do. It was so badly written, so tortuous I said to her, 'Well, are you going to vote?' She replied, 'I wouldn't vote for any of them'. So we threw it in the bin. I think that was the General Election when I was tempted to write 'stuff the lot' on the ballot paper and then I realized that we stuff the lotters would probably get a massive majority and the Queen would ring me up and ask me to form the next Government.

The demands of everyday life, not just work, are escalating. When I went to the United States I looked at some tests that they have of what was called 'minimal competency'. This is an attempt to try and identify those children who are going to have difficulties when they leave school and it was not just in maths and English, although those were important papers. There was one in life skills and the one I particularly liked was based on the guide to Yosemite State National Park. It was only when I looked through those questions that I realized how much people take for granted in terms of competence for something like leisure. We assume you can read, we assume you can understand a map, you can understand the symbols and you can do all this. If you cannot do so, you can still have recreation and leisure, but your choices are limited. So the world of the twenty-first century will make increased demands on people in their work. There will be very dramatically changed working patterns with perhaps much more re-training than we have had in previous ages. We are certainly going to see more demands on people in their family life. If they try to run a small business, there is no sign of that getting simpler; if anything it is getting more complex by the year. So that is one important message about the future, life will continue to become more complex.

There is another aspect of this and that is knowledge acquisition. Those of you who work in fields where you have to try and keep up-to-date in your own specialism, whatever it is, will know that it is very difficult with so much written, so much spoken, so much broadcast now of all kinds, about particular topics, science, technology, medicine, pollution, whatever it happens to be. That will be even more difficult to manage in the future and, although we have developed methods like computer-stored data bases, where you can retrieve information, I sympathize greatly with the Professor of Theology in my own university, who said in Senate, 'I don't want to retrieve information, I just want to read a book'. The file I most frequently use is called ERIC. It is the file on educational research in the Lockheed Dialog system which is based in Palo Alto in California, and it contains three hundred and fifty thousand different projects. Were I a physicist or a chemist or a biologist I would be consulting chemistry abstracts, biology previews and other files like that that have maybe two and a half million, three million or more research abstracts kept in them. We have three very clear messages for schools to-day. If children in the twenty-first century, when they are adults, are going to find the knowledge business even more complex, then message number one is 'If you cannot know everything, you have to know something'.

What, therefore, do we teach children at different ages? Hence the great argument about the National Curriculum and what should be in at various stages. But there is more to it than that. That is the first order question, but the second order question is, 'If you can't know everything, how to find out what you need to know?', and that involves being persistent, knowing where the sources of information are, being prepared to go to the library, look through the indexes, the bibliographies and so on, drag things out of hidden corners. The *process* in other words becomes important.

This brings me back to what is now rather a silly debate in education. From time to time someone will ring me up and say ,'Are you in favour of learning facts in history, or empathy?' and I say, 'Yes, of course', because again it is a silly question. How on earth can you empathize with a Roman soldier or a medieval peasant if you do not know any facts about that age, and equally if you know facts about that age, but do not have any understanding of what they really mean, then how on earth can you say you understand history. I never really understood some of the history I did until I read Professor W. G. Hoskins' book on 'lost villages'.[6] I was living in Leicestershire at the time and I went into these fields and got his little maps and there were the bumps in the fields. Suddenly the Enclosures Act, which was one of those torrents of things that one learned about in school with a date, the 'date-a-fact-a-line' approach, suddenly took on meaning. Here were people who were kicked off their land and some of them starved to death and others set off to London and never made it. Some of them made their home elsewhere. Here I was in this field having for the first time an understanding of what it all meant. I could never understand why the Romans were always going to the baths until I went to Rome. It is very hot in Rome, but nobody told me. There it was in Rome 90 plus temperature, everyone frantically trying to get cool, and then I went up to the Roman wall at Housesteads in Northumberland and wondered what lunatics built a swimming pool there.

In terms of the future, of course, children will need a terrific amount of *knowledge*, but they will need far more than that. First of all they also need *skills*. Not only do they need *knowledge* and *skills*, but also they need *attitudes* that go with them and they need to understand the *knowledge* and the *skills* and the *attitudes*. Ultimately the real test of quite a lot of learning is *behaviour*. What do people actually do?

I will give you a good example of that. In a field like health education, the real test of a health education programme is whether or not people actually lead healthy lives. It is no good teaching people about drug and solvent abuse if they then practise it. They have to know the facts. Sometimes they need certain skills like how to clean your teeth properly. My dentist is a great health educator. Mind you, he has got you strapped horizontally in a chair. Teachers envy that; he jacks you up to the ceiling and back down again when you first get in there just to show you who is in charge. Teachers do not have that kind of privilege; it is not in the Elton Report[7] anyway. He is a great health educator because he does not just give me the lecture on the aerodynamics of plaque, he actually sprays your teeth with this purple dye and says, 'Here's a toothbrush, now clean them'. Now I knew that horizontal brushing was out, and I thought that vertical brushing was in. But no, trendy dentists nowadays are into big circular movements you see, because the top of the tooth is shaped like a curve. I have now acquired a skill. It is not a marketable skill, but it is a skill. Then there is that matter of attitudes. Unless you really want to have good health you will not actually do the things you have learned about. But the ultimate test is behaviour— do you clean your teeth, do you have a healthy diet, do you avoid drugs and solvents and so on. So it is not as simple as saying the world of the twenty-first century is complex because there is a lot of knowledge to be learned and there are skills to be learned. People have to think about them, understand them, and develop positive attitudes.

Now to the third implication for schools. If number one is, 'You have to learn something', number two is 'You must learn how to find out', then number three is 'You have to learn to work with others'. Many of you are actually members of teams and if you were not good team members you would be a menace to your colleagues. If you are good team members it is a terrific bonus to your colleagues, because a group of people can work together more effectively than they could individually and that is one of the positive features of a good society, that people are willing to work together and put their skills at the disposal of others. Take the health care team in our health service. The doctor who treats you at home will probably not meet the consultant who sees you in a hospital. They will communicate by letter or by phone, and neither will meet the technician who analyses blood samples. But they are all part of a team and they have to have procedures whereby their expertise is made available to other members of the team. If they do that then the health care collectively available to you is better than you could get from individuals who worked entirely on their own. So the notion of working together with others becomes extremely important, an important value we need to have in our society.

I want now to come back from the future and look at the present, because to some extent I can see positive features of some of the developments that I have talked about. I think the fact that primary age children are now doing more science and technology is a very good development and I am delighted to see it. If ever you want to embark on a certain loser go and teach technology, because the syllabus is absolutely enormous. It covers design and technology, information technology, business studies and home economics and there is nobody alive as far as I can see has a grasp of all that lot, but if you really want to have your mind blown, go and teach it to 7-year-olds, as I did. I read the green folder and it tells you all about design ideas. You are supposed to generate the design ideas and then implement them. All I can say is that the group of 7-year-olds I worked with, who revolutionized the world with their design ideas, were only allowed to use round scissors. When you have just developed a marvellous idea for transforming humanity you discover that the Devon county rules say no child in an infant or first school may use sharp scissors. Devon has bought a job lot of round scissors which are specially designed not to cut. In fact, I suspect they were probably made in the pre-*glasnost* Soviet Union and any that did cut were thrown in the 'reject' box. The rest were packed neatly up and exported to Devon infant and first schools and so you cannot cut a thing. Nonetheless at least there is some decent technology going on now with children aged 7. Maybe they cannot implement all their ideas because they are not yet allowed to use power tools and Stanley knives, but there is an opportunity to develop some bright ideas which they may be able to implement later.

At least there is a chance to do physical science topics, like electricity, magnetism and so on, which often were not done. The HMI primary school survey[8] in the late 1970s, just after the Great Debate, said that in only one class in ten was there a decent science programme, but it also said that most of the science that was done was actually nature study, that there was very little physical science. It was mainly tadpoles and sticky buds and not too much electricity and magnetism forces and the topics that children are now doing. At Exeter we have just done another survey of 433 primary school teachers as part of the Leverhulme Primary Project and we found that teachers are now feeling more competent in science, though they are feeling less competent in all the other subjects. They are feeling more competent in science because they have been teaching it for the last two years and more competent in the process topics like helping children design an experiment to test a hypothesis.

I will say a little bit about the solutions to these concerns that we presently have. First of all about the National Curriculum. I like the individual bits of it. It sounds odd does it not, to say you like individual bits but you do not like the whole, because surely if you like the bits they must add up to a whole. But they do not and I think that is the problem. It is not surprising because, if you lock a few enthusiasts in a room and tell them that in the next three months or so they must produce a programme in their subject, is it surprising that they want the whole week? Lock away scientists, geographers, historians, art specialists whatever, they want the whole week for their particular discipline. So they produce these massive syllabuses. For those of you who are not perhaps familiar with the full range, in science for example there were originally seventeen attainment targets. I worked through them with a class of 7-year-olds when the National Curriculum first came out. I loved it, they loved it, but I did not know enough science. The range was quite enormous, because it was not only topics like the processes of life and electricity and magnetism and genetics and the uses of materials, which cover conventional chemistry, physics and biology, but there was astronomy, meteorology, earth sciences, an enormous range even for people who have graduated in some branch of science. Even in secondary schools, teachers with a major in biology find it difficult to teach all the physical science topics. They had to do some reading and find out more about them and so there was concern about that. It has now been reduced to five attainment targets but with much of the same content. So that has not actually made it easier to *teach*. It may make it easier to *assess* because there are fewer sub-headings, but it is the same content.

There is also an enormous amount in history. I really do like Key Stage 1 for 5- to 7-year-olds, because it simply says 'Who am I? What am I? Where am I?' Those of you who are teachers, and since it is Friday afternoon, will know that is exactly how you feel. But Key Stage 2 contains all the invaders and settlers, the Romans, the Saxons, the Normans, the Egyptians and the Greeks, the building technology of the pyramids and the Parthenon, the Aztecs, the routes to the Spice Islands, wherever they are, the Tudors and Stuarts, Victorian social history, the history of plough design, and the one that I felt was really over the top, the history of transport before and after the wheel. When that particular document came out in imperial purple, as you probably remember, about a couple of years ago, I was talking at a conference in Keele where there were about four hundred teachers. I went through those topics and they were rolling in the aisles 'He's a lad isn't he, making this stuff up?' I said 'No it is all statutory now and it is hello Strangeways if you don't teach it'. You can take it from me the next generation of people on Strangeways roof throwing tiles will actually be teachers who have been locked up for not teaching the history National Curriculum and are protesting that they cannot get hold of a copy of Trevelyan.

Exactly the same applies to geography. In our most recent survey we found that, whereas teachers were most anxious about science and technology two years ago when we surveyed them, now they are most concerned about geography and history, because they have seen the syllabuses: 54 per cent of teachers said they felt competent with their existing subject knowledge in history two years ago and that has now gone down to 38 per cent. Geography has gone down by an equal amount because people have now seen how full these syllabuses are and again I say it is not surprising because, to their great credit, the enthusiasts who were shut away to do this exercise were very keen to get in as much as possible. In fact there is a hilarious story about the geography committee, which you probably know, which was that Kenneth Baker wanted an explorer to chair it. Of course, if there is one genus of people who are not sitting at the end of a phone waiting to be asked to chair a government committee it is explorers. Explorers are out exploring. I suddenly had this ludicrous image of Kenneth Baker wading neck deep up the Limpopo looking for an explorer, pursued by a dozen television crews. In the end they got a Vice Chancellor to chair it, on the grounds presumably that he, at least, was at home.

The science curriculum has earth sciences in it, but then so does geography because it is physical geography and, because the two committees worked independently of each other, they could not talk to each other. Maths has overlap with other subjects as well. This was bound to happen. I think we are going to have to do what every other country does, which is to thin it out and get it down to a single pamphlet so that people can actually look through it and see what it is, rather than have to look at twenty or thirty or more folders and booklets.

Then there is the question of testing. Again it is far too complex and the real nightmare is going to be testing at Key Stage 3: 14-year-olds. Look at the mayhem we had with 7-year-olds. I am strongly in favour of testing, but not of what we are doing, because what we are trying to do is devise one single kind of test which will meet every aspiration and there is not such a test. If you know anything about testing technology you will know that teachers assess in different ways, sometimes very informally, sometimes by talking to someone, raising an eyebrow, smiling, nodding. Most of the assessment that goes on in class is actually like that. The ritualized, once a year or end of term or every month test or the weekly spelling test is a minority of the actual assessment that goes on, so we have many informal procedures available. We also have 'when-ready' type tests. If you decide that a certain child is at a certain point in October and you want to check if he can do tens and units, multiply two 2-digit numbers, you may as well set two or three examples in October rather than having to wait until April or May.

It is quite legitimate to say that parents want to know how their children are getting on. Teachers need to know what children can and cannot do. Employers or anybody else hiring people need to know what someone can do. We also need to know how schools compare with each other. We need to know how authorities compare with each other. All legitimate demands. We need to know whether we are getting better as a nation. Are we any better now at reading than we were back in 1976? We need to know about this. It is useful to know. But there is no single test that will do all those things. Take reading. Among the 7-year-olds I am currently teaching, if I wanted to know how a particular child was reading I would actually say, for starters, 'Go and get a book that you have been reading recently and read it to me.' I would then be able to make judgements: should this child be on a higher book? Is the child struggling and should s/he be given something a bit simpler, coming on to this kind of book later? So 'Bring me a book you are currently reading' is not a bad informal diagnostic kind of test. But it is utterly useless if you want to compare one year with the next, because one child will bring you *War and Peace* and the other will bring you *Little Twinky Rides Again*. If you want to compare one year with another you need standardized tests, and they are different very often from diagnostic tests which build up profiles.

Think of the mayhem we had testing 7-year-olds on three levels of the National Curriculum levels 1, 2 and 3, on three subjects, Maths, Science and English and on nine attainment targets. Now go forward to 14-year-olds doing ten subjects, potentially at ten levels. There will be 14-year-olds on level 1 and there will be 14-year-olds on level 10; there is no doubt about that. Assessment is important, but how important? Who needs to know and how much time is it worth investing in it? If we can get that right there will not be one murmur of dissent from the teaching profession about assessing, apart from a tiny, tiny minority that like to believe that they never assess at all. I remember one teacher—it was a head actually—who said, 'I have never assessed a child in my life' and I said 'I don't believe it, I don't believe you have never smiled, never nodded, never raised an eyebrow, never said "good". You may not have sat down with a formal test, but you have done it.'

Finally, let me just say a little bit about what I think is the way ahead. I am not at all happy about the market view of education. I echo what Lord Callaghan said about this. I go back to what I said earlier about life in the future. We are going to have to work together in teams, and I strongly support that notion. For me, one of the joys of working in education has been seeing schools collaborating with each other in friendly rivalry. There is a lot of collaboration, joint in-service work, teachers coming together for various things, like the Technical and Vocational Education Initiative (TVEI), for a very good example. Everywhere where TVEI took place there were consortia of schools that got together and shared ideas. There are consortia of schools in rural areas, trying to work out how to teach the National Curriculum in a small school and that is one of the great bonuses of life in a profession like teaching, that you can work with other professional people, because it can be a lonely job if you do not.

But what is going to happen when league tables come and the feeling you have is that, if you help the school down the road, they may end up higher on the league table than you and you will then be regarded as not being too good, so a few parents will defect and you will have less money. One or two teachers then leave because you cannot afford to pay them and therefore you cannot afford as many books and pieces of equipment and so your results get a bit worse and you are caught in a downward spiral, not because you are no good, but because you are teaching in difficult circumstances and you are willing to collaborate rather than engage in cut-throat competition. I think we will have lost something if we have that.

Secondly, I do not believe in what the present government is doing in another respect. Lord Joseph stayed up half the night in the House of Lords trying to talk out the National Curriculum. It got very little reporting, but he actually stayed up until 2 or 3 in the morning arguing against a National Curriculum. He argued against a National Curriculum on grounds that I would not have done, even though I had some reservations about it; he argued on market grounds. If you want schools to compete with each other then you actually should leave them free to choose their own curriculum. Why tie them down, or why tie some of them down, because the independent schools did not have to do it? What I do not like is that we neither have got a pure market nor do we have the kind of collaboration that I would like to see. We have something in between that is neither.

Although I am very critical of the present government's education policies, I would give them some credit for a number of things, but I would give them no credit at all for the favouring of the semi-independent sector, which I think is quite wrong. City Technology Colleges are being given £7 million, £8 million, £9 million for a new building. Grant-maintained schools are also unfairly favoured. One in our area that opted out was given £850,000 for a new building. The going rate in our county for buildings is about £15,000 to £20,000 per school. Nobody believes, I am sure, that if everybody opted out the government would quadruple or quintuple the money for school buildings. Kenneth Clarke said in January that there was no favouring of grant-maintained schools, but then John Major said in August that they were favouring grant-maintained schools because they wanted more to opt out and they were therefore giving them more money for capital building. Now I think that that is not straight, honest market dealing. Even by its own criteria, if there is a market you let the market go, you let it rip, you do not give some of the competitors, so to speak, a government provided sports car and then tie the ankles of the others to the starting gate. I think it is morally wrong, and the government should be ashamed of itself on that; it leaves a deep scar.

I am against the market because for another reason, I do not think it works in the terms it is supposed to work. In my own field in higher education, we were told that in-service training is now a market. You provide and you get customers and therefore, if you do not compete with other providers, no one will come and you will not make any money. Actually in my university, as in many, we subsidize in-service training. We do it because we like it, because we get on well with teachers. We know that they like us go into schools, doing school-based in-service work. We think we have something to offer, but we also know we learn a lot when we do work with teachers in schools because they tell us at first-hand and we see at first-hand and we often teach in their own schools anyway. So it is a great partnership and we do not see it as a money-making thing at all. If I telephone a colleague of mine at Hong Kong University he would recruit me ten Hong Kong students at £4000 fees a time tomorrow. That is making money in the market and we do not want to play that sort of game. There are many other examples of how the market will not serve the customers it is intended to serve and I include here right at the centre the children themselves, because if resources drain away from a school through market forces there will be many thousands of children, as Lord Callaghan mentioned, marooned in impoverished schools that desperately need all they can get. One of the great programmes that we had throughout the 1970s, like Project Headstart in the United States, was the Educational Priority Area scheme where we actually said 'These children are up against it, so let's give them extra'.

What happens in the present climate is that people become subversive. I wrote a jokey column in the *Times Educational Supplement* a couple of weeks ago about a head talking to Mr Ramsbottom, the chairman of governors and saying, 'I have tried to improve our A-Level statistics. I only entered the two children who passed the mock exams, so this year we went up to 50 per cent'. People will do that; people will find out how the league table is assembled. If it is assembled on the number of high-grade GCSEs, then take all the clever pupils and put them in for three more subjects. They will probably pass them and if they do not it does not matter; they will get one or two. At least it will help the batting average. So if you then change the criterion to overall pass rates, schools will not enter pupils unless they are absolutely certain to pass. I will tell you two stories from the United States. I went to a school in San Diego which had gone testing mad; the staff seemed to spend all their time predicting children's test scores, giving tests, scoring them and entering the scores on to the sheets. It was far worse that we have had, because it went on all year and this to me was the ultimate nightmare. I went into the head's study and she had all round her room hundreds of blue folders absolutely crammed full of children's profiles on numerous discrete behavioural type objectives. 'Can blend phonemes' was one. You had to predict whether Mavis would be able to blend phonemes in the coming semester; then you had to test Mavis to find out whether or not she could blend phonemes and then you had to enter it all in the record, and there were dozens of these. The principal of the school had to countersign them. So I said to her, 'Do you use these?' she said 'Oh it's built into our contract, you know. If we don't do it we can be fired and, as principal, if I haven't countersigned every one of those books and someone comes in from the School Board I can be dismissed'. So I said, 'Yes I know that, but do you use them?' She said, 'What do you mean?' So I said, 'Do you ever take them down and say 'Look we thought Mavis would be blending phonemes by Christmas, now it's April and she hasn't even found the blender.' She said, 'Good Lord no, we are so exhausted from filling the forms in, the last thing we want to do is to take them out again.'

So that is one nightmare, but the second nightmare is pure subversion. I was attending the American Educational Research Association conference and I was talking to an academic I had known for many years who had been looking at the test scores in every single American state where they published their scores and then comparing them with the national average. You will be delighted to hear that every state in America scores above the national average and I think that one way or another we will have that sort of league table subversion.

Lord Callaghan started off a very important debate. I think he started it off in a very effective way. Prime ministers do not often make speeches about education; they tend to concentrate on foreign policy, economic matters and the great affairs of state, but relatively rarely go into the field of education. It came at the right time when there was concern that was not always being expressed, when there was a need for more lay interest, because we were in danger of people becoming apathetic, because they felt excluded. It came at a critical time in our history when we were beginning to face significant unemployment, and that was a shock for many people because it seemed to be something in the past and now we were seeing it in the present and the future.

For fifteen years there has been a debate. I think some of it has been very good, but some of it has been absolutely awful. We have seen some significant improvements and sadly teachers have not always been given the credit for these, such as for example the improvement in examination results. It was very interesting when A-Levels were taken this year, the predictions in the press were that it would be a disaster; it was the first GCSE cohort. Then very quietly, when the results came out there was a little footnote on page 93 that said, 'Oh, by the way, the results were one per cent better than last year.' But then there was an article the following week to say they probably fixed them anyway. Now that is not fair. It is not fair to treat education that way. There should be honest reporting of education.

When the report on the Assessment of Performance Units testing of children in Maths from 1984–88,[9] came out recently, what it showed was that, in the five areas where they tested, scores had actually gone down in only one—number, which was bad news, because number is very important in adult life. It is virtually the only maths that most people do. But scores had gone up in measures, probability/statistics, geometry, algebra; in four out of five areas 11-year-old scores had gone up. Now a good report on that would have said, 'Well done, eight out of ten, but number, that's disastrous, we have got to do something about that.' No teacher in the land would object to that kind of reaction to education. I think that is what Lord Callaghan wanted when he started the debate and I think that is what John MacGregor wanted when he talked about HMI reports, saying, 'Well done on some things, but now look into others'.

For me, not just because I work in it, education is absolutely vital. Lord Callaghan recognized that when he said the things he said in 1976. It is all our future and I have often said this, because I believe it and not just to keep my own spirits up. But I believe if a Martian landed in our society now, seeing us heading for the turmoil of greater complexities, an exciting challenge but nonetheless confusing, not able to see yet where we are going in this present post-industrial revolution, what he would say is, 'Education and training are vitally important. All those people who work in the education service, primary teachers, secondary teachers, tertiary, further, higher education teachers, the advisers, administrators, HMI are very important people in a society that is rapidly moving.' That keeps me going and I hope it keeps you going too.

NOTES

1. National Youth Employment Council (1974) *The Unqualified, Untrained and Unemployed*. London: HMSO.
2. DES (1978) *Primary Education in England: A Survey by HMI*. London: HMSO.
3. DES (1979) *Aspects of Secondary Education in England*. London: HMSO.
4. Wragg, E.C. (1980) 'State-approved knowledge ? Ten steps down the slippery slope', in Golby, M. (ed.) *The Core Curriculum* (Perspectives 2, pp. 11–20). Exeter: University of Exeter.
5. Toffler, A. (1970) *Future Shock*. London: Bodley Head.
6. Hoskins, W.G. (1950) 'The Deserted Villages of Leicestershire', in *Essays in Leicestershire History*. Liverpool: Liverpool University Press.
7. DES/WO (1989) *Committee of Enquiry into Discipline in Schools* (The Elton Report). London: HMSO.
8. See note 2.
9. School Examinations and Assessment Council (1991) *APU Mathematics Monitoring 1984–88 (Phase 2)* Slough, NFER

Part 2

Chapter 5

Retrospect on Ruskin: Prospect on the 1990s

John Tomlinson

James Callaghan announced a political agenda in October 1976 which remained salient until 1986—broadly, the period of Shirley Williams, Mark Carlisle and Keith Joseph; from Ruskin to *Better Schools*.[1] Moreover, that political agenda for education resonated in many important respects with a suppressed professional agenda so that they reinforced one another. Then, in the third period of Conservative government, a sharp New Right agenda was imposed through the 1988 Education Reform Act and the 1989 Local Government Act. The fundamental purposes of this were to transfer power from providers to consumers and to reintroduce a selective system of secondary education through the creation of a market in schooling.

The effects are still being worked through as we plunge into the 1990s. I intend to show that it has put the service in a totally inappropriate position; we are facing 180° the wrong way if we are to meet the real needs of the economy and society now emerging. The period since James Callaghan's speech has therefore been one in which some valuable reorientation and change of attitudes took place; but the imposition of a political dogma in the closing stages means that yet further change will be needed.

I will go through the history since 1976 in a little more detail in a moment. But that will make more sense and my position will be more clear, if I immediately explain what kind of society and economy I think is emerging—has already been established in many respects—and how that connects with the kind of school system we need.

WHAT KIND OF SOCIETY?

There is general agreement that Britain, like many 'Western societies', has moved from a normative to a pluralist society. Somewhere in the 1950s and 1960s—round about *That Was the Week That Was*—we shed strong forces of conformity and deference which had provided a social structure of a kind: class, religion, 'respect for one's betters' and the Reithian sense of propriety; the unwritten codes, respect for the strong, normative institutions. In their place we have created a society in which different religions and creeds—from the most authoritarian to the most nihilistic—and different forms of lifestyle are deemed equally valid and worthy of respect in the public forum. Late nineteenth-century liberalism created a society in which there was a great deal of personal freedom (for those with resources to exercise it) amid tight social structures. We have chosen to bring these personal freedoms into the public domain, and most of the social structure has dissolved.

As Jonathan Sacks puts it so vividly in the 1990 Reith lectures: 'The problem is that pluralism gives rise to deep and intractable conflicts while undermining the principles by which they might be resolved. It disintegrates our concept of the common good.'[2]

It is well known that the transition from liberalism to pluralism has 'bouleversed' the schools. From being a large cog in the mechanism by which norms and codes were transmitted they have become the cockpit in which the conflicts are first encountered by the young. Not understanding the nature of the pathology, the far right wing calls for more (Christian) religious observance and the teaching of citizenship; the far left urges a treacly toleration, mixed with sporadic pursuit of newly identified injustices. Neither is intellectually or spiritually satisfying.

Let me leave the issue of pluralism there for the moment and look at another aspect of our changing society—a society that has gone 'beyond the stable state' and where change not stability is the norm.

The so-called 'knowledge society' has long been foretold and seems seriously to be appearing. In the knowledge society, the predominant factor of production is human capital, and particularly the knowledge and skill of each individual. It is the exact opposite of factory mass production in which individuals do similar things and are under close supervision. It places the individual in a position of extraordinary power, power which can be used to influence or distort the lives of others, even though those others themselves will be equally powerful in their own field of work. It has the potential for sophisticated anarchy.

To complete the trio of forces working towards concentration on the significance of the individual, I would cite the new paradigm of science, the end of the crudities perpetrated in the name of the mechanistic view of the universe of Descartes and Newton. It has been recognized that if we are to survive as a species then the use of science to exploit the planet must be brought under control. Science must return to where the Greeks had it: as wisdom. Polities, as the instruments of a democratic will, must be able to control individuals and corporations.

MORAL RESPONSIBILITY

Where do these three trends lead us? They all, in my view, reveal that the quality of our life, indeed the possibility of its survival, will depend on the sense of moral responsibility of the individual. In the pluralist society, once we have removed the moral and social glue of conformity, only the individual can provide a substitute. In the knowledge society, where individuals have the power of knowledge, only their individual moral impulse stands between use and abuse. And on a fragile planet the attitude of the individual to ecological imperatives will, ultimately, determine whether the species survives.

There is now a considerable body of writing which supports this kind of analysis. Peter Drucker in *The New Realities*[3] argues that 'society dominated by knowledge-workers makes ever newer—and ever more stringent—demands for social performance and social responsibility...education in moral values, and the commitment to moral values, will have to be central. Knowledge and knowledge people have to take responsibility' (pp. 224 and 230). And in her striking book *Cognitive Apprenticeships*, Lauren Resnick makes the same essential point.[4] So does Zuboff in *The Age of the Smart Machine: The Future of Work and Power*.[5]

In the pluralistic society, ever tending towards greater fragmentation, only the moral force of the individual will hold communities and the wider society together. It is striking that, long before academics began to see this truth those working in the arts had seen it. For example in *Women in Love*, D.H. Lawrence, in the argument between Gerald and Birkin, made clear the new imperative towards taking personal responsiblity. (I quoted it in my address to the North of England Conference in 1978 to illustrate the point I am making again now—it is part of the underlying agenda of this half-century.)

In those circumstances it is clear that education should attend not only to the instrumental and the academic. It must also play a crucial part in conveying to the young the necessary sense of personal responsibility towards others and the world of nature generally. Moreover, I suggest, such education will only take root if it is done within a genuine experience of social cohesion. The school must be a moral community, continually exploring the ethics of the common life. By that I mean a life in which all are valued, all are expected to contribute and all are helped to contribute. Note, it is *not* a society in which all are expected to be able to do the same or are required to become the same. Good education is about the creation of unique identities yet within a matrix of fraternity.

And it is not only analysis of the nature of society which leads to the necessity for education to provide for individual responsiblity and social cohesion. I could argue in the mid-1980s— following the NEDO report Competence and Competition,[6] Ernest Gellner and others—that a mobile and highly differentiated labour force to be effective must share a common culture. A modern economy is hampered by deep social and class divisions. In advanced societies education is expected to provide 'not only the skills required...but [also] the qualities of social integration which are a pre-condition of their use.'[7] And in 1990, Sir Colin Marshall, Chief Executive of British Airways, diagnosed the British economic problem as being structural and systemic: social immobility and institutional rigidity lay at the heart of British under-achievement.[8] Sir John Harvey-Jones and others have echoed the same argument.

THE AGENDA FOR SCHOOLS

Here then, I argue, is the true agenda that the schools of Britain have to follow in the 1990s, in recognition of our pluralistic society, the imperatives of the emergent knowledge society and the need not only for knowledge and skills to fuel our economy but a greater sense of common goals and the experience of social cohesion in order to optimize their use. I do not, for a moment, argue that the schools are the only force that should be working this way or that they could possibly succeed if every other aspect of society was working within a contrary value system. Of course they could not. It has been the imposition of contradictory self-defeating demands of that kind in the past which has bedevilled the schools and caused some of their loss of esteem.

Chelly Halsey pointed out 20 years ago[9] that 'there has been a tendency to treat education as the waste-paper basket of social policy—a repository for dealing with social problems where solutions are uncertain or where there is a disinclination to wrestle with them seriously. Such problems are prone to be dubbed 'educational' and turned over to the schools to solve.'

Of course, the schools cannot do it alone. But I do argue that the education of our young is a prime means by which we can, as a society, help to realize those values we hold dear. The curriculum of schools, in its public statement, is a description of the kind of society we want to become. If we could have *that* kind of National Curriculum, we might both end the national game of making schools the scapegoats and achieve something of great value instead.

DEVELOPMENTS SINCE RUSKIN

Now, let us examine where we have reached by 1991 as a result of all the turmoil since Ruskin. And let us see which of the aspirations and systems we have in place might help us to tackle the agenda I have identified and which are inimical.

I said earlier that I thought that the ideas of the Ruskin speech had not only signalled a political agenda which lasted a decade, but also released a professional agenda and by that I mean the ideas and aspirations of teachers and administrators that had been suppressed or derided by the inertia of the formal academic tradition and the vested interests attached to them. Callaghan said that schools should pay more attention to preparing pupils for working life, reconsider curriculum and teaching methods and be more willing to share power with parents. He also called for a core curriculum, a more interventionist role for the DES and HM Inspectorate, and more lay influence on and through governing bodies. The background to this intervention by a Prime Minister included the Black Papers (which had started, it must be remembered, as early as 1969),[10] the economic crisis from 1973 and the desire of DES officials to strengthen their role, particularly following the criticisms of the OECD report[11] which had said they were not active enough in planning the education system. The DES position was summed up in the 'Yellow Book' of July 1976, its response to Downing Street's request for a view of the education scene. It was followed faithfully in the Ruskin speech.

Once it was accepted that curriculum should be discussed more openly and that new 'stakeholders' should be admitted, once the Taylor Committee had suggested broadening the membership of school governing bodies, once the connection between education and the world of work had been accepted, and once it had been admitted that new forms of education required new methods of teaching and assessment, then a strong professional body of opinion surfaced and found a voice. It is very doubtful whether the changes in curriculum, teaching, assessment and organization achieved in the period 1976-85 could have gone so far without this confluence of political and professional thinking. It is one of the ironies of a period in which, increasingly, professional thinking and leadership were denigrated and set at low value by politicians. Nonetheless I suggest that most of the reforms up to and including those proposed in *Better Schools*[12] were actually drawn from the stock of ideas existing by the late 1970s. They owed their existence to a number of sources. The curriculum movement since the 1960s had tackled questions of how schools and teachers can be helped to understand, accept and carry forward innovation. The school improvement movement had shown the importance of seeing schools as whole systems and thinking of their management as consisting of the interaction of curriculum development, staff development and organizational development. Facing the raising of the school leaving age had forced attention on questions of curricula and methods based in experiential learning and new forms of student motivation. The Education for Capability campaign, conceived in the mid-1970s, and which embraced many outside education as well as many within it, encapsulated a powerful strand of the thinking of the New Education:

There is a serious imbalance in Britain today in the full process which is described by the two words 'education' and 'training'...[which] is harmful to individuals, to industry and to society. A well-balanced education should, of course, embrace analysis and the acquisition of knowledge. But it must also include the exercise of creative skills, the competence to undertake and complete tasks and the ability to cope with everyday life; and also doing all these things in co-operation with others.[13]

A month before the Ruskin speech, at another college in Oxford, a few HMIs, LEA administrators and teachers met together and planned a whole-school curriculum development and review project which was to lead directly to the influential Red Books on *Curriculum 11–16*[14] (1977–83) and indirectly to *Curriculum Matters 2, The Curriculum 5–16*[15] and thence to the better ideas of the National Curriculum.

The period 1976–85 was therefore one of considerable innovation in curriculum, assessment (the GCSE, records of achievement, criterion-referenced tests) and in-school organization, where much valuable ground was gained.

THE 1980s

But we must now turn to the debit side of the balance sheet. Although the government of the 1980s kept the agenda announced by Callaghan they pursued it by new methods informed by different values. And then they added completely alien items. By the end of the decade the medium had nearly stifled the message.

At first, from 1979–85, it was the methods not the objectives that were new. Those methods produced an acceleration effect it is most unlikely would have been possible under any government that continued to use the traditional tools of consultation and consensus. Consultative bodies were disbanded and procedures compressed—often into the summer holidays to the intended discomfort of teachers and local authority associations. Where new consultative or executive machinery was created, its members were not appointed to represent a range and balance of interests but were nominated by government. Underlying these processes were deeper objectives of the neo-liberal programme, namely removing or neutralizing institutions and power groupings which intervene between the state and the individual, notably the breaking of the power of the teachers' trade unions (over pay, conditions of service and curriculum), a significant reduction in the powers of local government and its realignment towards being an agency of central government, together with an orchestrated denigration of the teaching profession. Because the teachers' associations claimed interest in professional standards as well as trade union activity, it was possible to attack the professionalism of teachers at the same time as their trade unions. In this latter respect above all, Sir Keith Joseph's prescription broke with the Callaghan approach. Callaghan had said, 'We must carry the teaching profession with us'. These factors and the long and bitter teachers' pay dispute of 1984–87 softened up both public opinion and the 'educational establishment' for a complete break with tradition. There was no longer any expectation that a consensus would be sought and therefore no need to seek one. Moreover, by the mid-1980s a good deal of the work of the schools was subject to earmarked grant from central government, a device which simultaneously marginalized the LEAs and began the forging of the tools of direct central control of schools. In some cases the grant came from a department other than DES, so that schools and LEAs were subject to an incongruent variety of regimes and value sets. The grant usually involved a management contract and pre-determined performance criteria. Creativity arising from the process of innovation itself was neither expected nor encouraged. The Technical and Vocational Education Initiative (TVEI) derived from the Manpower Services Commission (Department of Employment), Mini Enterprises in School from the Department of Trade and Industry. A range of curriculum projects was funded by DES Education Support Grants and in-service training largely paid for by DES grants with the plans subject to prior DES approval.

In short, by 1986, a system which for 35 years, until 1970, had been run through broad legislative objectives, convention and consensus had been replaced by one based on contract and management.

Thus by 1986 the stage had been set for the radical phase of neo-conservative educational policy. Although there were some deliberate leaks, the manifesto of 1987, which provided the 'mandate' for the 1988 Reform Act, was prepared in secret during the previous nine months under the general direction of the Prime Minister's Policy Unit. The aim was to make an irreversible change in the public education system, similar to that already achieved in other aspects of social and economic policy, such as trade union legislation, the sale of council houses, and the privatization of nationalized industries.

THE 1988 EDUCATION ACT

The results are well known and I will not detail them but state and analyse some of the underlying objectives. The 1988 Education Act, of course, contained both 'old' and 'new' Conservative thinking. The drive towards centralization continued. By 1990 the school curriculum, assessments at 7, 11, 14 and 16, all public examinations, the initial teacher training curriculum, in-service training, teacher appraisal, teachers' pay and conditions, capital building and the formulae for fixing individual school budgets, to mention only the obvious, were all directly under the control of central government. It is a breathtaking list not to be found in any other modern state.

But the free market lobby triumphed as well as the centralizers. The conditions for promoting a market in schooling were created. To have a market there must be distinctly different kinds of school from which parents can choose, hence city technology colleges, grant-maintained schools and the extension and additional funding of the assisted places scheme for independent schools. Within the LEA maintained sector, open enrolment and individual school budgets were used to encourage schools to compete with one another.

We are, I believe, at the cusp of this process. If the next government continues to encourage the market by subsidizing opting-out and inter-school competition, the process may be irreversible. In that case, we shall have abandoned any attempt to see the schools of the country as a coherent public system working collectively and consciously towards the connection between public education and the public good.

THE MARKET IN EDUCATION

I believe further that this will be an error of stupendous proportions. Two kinds of criticism can be levelled at the use of a market to distribute educational opportunity and are now strongly emerging in the literature. At the instrumental level of merely achieving the objectives set for it by government, the market approach will fail. There will be far more failing schools and under-educated children than in the previous, however imperfect, planned system. And far, far more failing schools than there would be in a system informed by the best of our current knowledge of how to promote and to manage successful schools and do so within a publicly accountable system. So we shall not reap the educated citizens every commentator and political party says we need.

At a deeper level, we shall not achieve the objectives that are to be derived from my opening analysis of the pluralistic society and the emergent knowledge society.

The way in which a market in school education will fail has been well analysed—for example in the IPPR pamphlet, *Markets, Politics and Education*.[16] It is a false analogy to say that because independent schools operate in a market all schools can. Independent schools choose which pupils to accept and the scale of their operation (most choose stability of size). Schools in a system intended for all children are required to admit those who seek entry and are a totally different case. If they choose to be selective they merely pass on the difficulties, in aggravated form, to other schools. Good schools will be threatened with overcrowding and short-term oscillations in size; other schools will have to stay open during a period of declining resources where teachers and pupils will find conditions deteriorating and yet not within their control to improve—the exact opposite of the theoretical market mechanism. The decisions of a few parents about choice of school will affect the education and life chances of the children of a far greater number of other parents. And that will be true in both those schools deemed successful and those being shunned.

Moreover, and equally undesirable, the inter-school systems of co-operation and mutual support, so carefully developed, will be attacked by the ethos of competition and the LEA-wide services for minority groups, special needs, in-service training and curriculum development will attenuate or close as more and more funds are transferred to the schools. Governors of individual schools will make decisions in the interests of that school alone, not in the interests of a wider system or other schools, of which they can have no knowledge and for which they carry no responsibility. The notion that the aggregrate of individual school decisions to draw upon supra-school services could support a viable service in laughable.

The end of the road, and the stated objective of some who advocated it, is a system sharply differentiated in several respects. There will be a selective privatized sector much larger than the 5 per cent or so typical since 1944. There will be a direct-grant sector, increasingly selective in character. There will be an LEA sector in prosperous areas gaining significant funding from parents beyond the publicly provided school budget. And there will be a remnant public sector, serving areas already suffering multiple deprivation and representing a history of failure in public policies for generations, where the schools will be expected to 'educate' an underclass. Whether such schools, as they increasingly emerge, will be able to attract staff must be problematic. The market could represent a decision to abandon the promises of 1902 and 1944 of 'education for all'. It would underline the remark of a government minister in the early 1980s that the country has never afforded to give all its people a decent education.

WHAT KIND OF SOCIETY?

I return to the kind of issues I raised at the beginning. What kind of society does the 1988 Education Act envisage? We were never told. What fundamental purposes is society expecting its maintained schools to pursue in this new future? The clumsy and inappropriate sections on religious observance were inserted under duress and as an after-thought; the debate on citizenship arose after the event, through the Speaker's Conference and the Prince's Trust. Neither has led to a coherent outcome.

The language of discourse in education has changed profoundly over the decade. Education is clearly seen as a tool of economic policy and of new kinds of social policy. 'Maintaining a competitive edge' seems categorically inferior as a national objective when compared with earlier aspirations towards a liberal education or greater social justice. It is a phenomenon known to policy analysts as the reversal of means and ends.[17]

The pure neo-liberal answer to such problems is clearly inadequate. To say that choices in the market will produce a more satisfactory result and that all will be better off, even though differences will be greater, simply does not address the right question. How, in an individualistic, competitive society, do you get enough 'moral and social glue' to keep things together—to attain even Nozick's minimalist state?

Are we aiming for a minimalist morality in which you do good (or avoid doing harm) to others only if it is in your own interests? And do those who may advocate that believe, therefore, that we have solved the ancient philosophical problem of how to devise moral imperatives from contractarian ethics? If so, it would be news to many of us. Let us hear the case.

Or are we saying that there are other and higher moral principles that should inform human life? And are some of these directly related to the new realities I have pointed out, the pluralistic, atomized society, the knowledge society and our ecological vulnerability?

The nub of the problem is this. The philosophy of individualism, at least since the seventeenth century, has contained two different moral teachings and the difference is starkly unresolved in current educational policy. Mrs Thatcher gave the General Assembly of the Church of Scotland one view—that of Thomas Hobbs. The unseen country of the spirit grows soul by soul, not through social interaction. In this sense there *is* no such thing as society. Another view, expressed in the tradition of Edmund Burke and John Stuart Mill, is that 'men and women are social beings'.[18] The first tradition, though denounced in the nineteenth century and thought by some to be dead, still flourishes and puts rights before duties. 'It treats society as a mere association of individuals who owe nothing to others.'[19] The other tradition, a 'republican individualism' puts duties alongside or before rights. Like Kant's moral philosophy of the categorical imperative, it is the kind of individualism which is no threat to morality or civic duty.

SCHOOLS AS COMMUNITIES

Schools cannot avoid being moral communities: any kind of human association requires an ethic. The question arising from the conflicts and contradictions in current policy which I have identified is what kind of moral community are we requiring them to be? The pressures appear to be towards social Darwinism. Is that what even those who support the policy wanted? And, if we look more deeply into ourselves as individuals and members of the communities and workplaces of Britain, is it what we need?

I hope I have convinced you that whatever the practical gains in clarification of curriculum, school organization and public accountability that were made in the 1980s—and I support them—the underlying mechanism of the Education Reform Act and its successive regulation is the exact opposite of what we need. What we need is a publicly accountable education service (and a service is much more than the individual schools) dedicated to explicit notions of the public good.

I am clear what I want to see. I want a schools system where access is determined solely by being a citizen of this country—not on grounds of wealth, or birth, or race or sex or religion; and I want those schools to pursue the ideal of the common school by providing an experience for all their pupils that is at the same time life-enhancing for the individuals and socially cohesive.

Fine words, you may say. What hope is there of really achieving them? Far far more than our politicians have any vision of. The desperate plight we are in is caused not by the low aspirations of our people but by the low aspirations of our leaders. If only it was understood what so many schools and LEAs have aspired to and achieved we would be planning for yet greater success not for radical reshaping.

It is as though the difficulties and striving of some schools in the most dismal of circumstances had been read as the condition of all 25,000. It as as though the dedication, grinding hard work and faith in human potential shown by the vast majority of those working in the service had never been seen, far less understood or accepted. Instead, the debate has been conducted at the most superficial levels of information, intellectual acuity and political theory.

Once the education service and those working in it were seen as the problem, then all aspects of existing and previous education effort were stigmatized. Can it be even remotely likely, on any historical precedent you care to suggest, that that could be true? And is an atavistic pining for past simplicities and 'educational basics' remotely likely to serve the needs of a society aspiring to be a successful high-technology innovative economy and the political leader of wider communities in the twenty-first century?

All the ideas and most of the systems we need have already been invented, most of them in the UK. Their applications, like so much invented here, are being realized abroad.

CREATING LEARNING COMMUNITIES

At the root of the new thinking—by which I mean the development of the best of the old thinking—is the idea of creating learning communities. Sadly the phase is in danger of becoming hackneyed before it has even been understood, much less realized on any scale. The principles of such learning communities are easily stated:

1. There are many more ways to teach and learn than was the case even a generation ago. Each has a value for a purpose or process, but the match needs careful thought and organization.

2. Many such processes of learning are based on new technologies. And by that I do not mean merely the computer for calculation and word processing but the richness now available or potential in art, design, music, drama and symbolism of many kinds.

3. Such learning and teaching has two key characteristics:

   a. It involves the learner in new ways and therefore also changes the teacher.

   b. It goes on outside formal institutions of education and training as well as within them.

4. Therefore the learning community is the whole community in which the youngster is growing up. Unless that community is engaged the results will be unsatisfactory. Engage them, draw

upon the richness of people and locality, and the results are astonishing as so many schools have already shown. There is a saying in Africa that 'it takes a whole village to educate a child'.

5. Such learning can provide all the 'basics' of knowledge as transmitted information, but also conveys so much more as knowledge-learned-in-experience. Moreover, the confidence, a sense of personal responsibility, the ability to work in a team or group so prized in the world outside schools, grows as well.

I know of schools that have glimpsed these aspirations and are working towards them. In the process they are growing as self-critical, self-developing human organizations. And they are also engaging with those around them, parents, employers, voluntary organizations, significant individuals in many fields of life. They are both empowering and using the power of their communities. In such a milieu, life-long learning for the adults, training for workplace or private ambition, the transition from school to adult and working life, are all accepted as components, not bolt-on extras or bright new ideas imposed from outside. So many of the ideas of the 1980s, such as the Schools Curriculum Award, or Education 2000, or the GRASP approach to learning have shown the way. Their teaching has been all but ignored by government and their gifts and those of so many others are in danger of being squandered. They will have to be reinvented after the passage through the desert, if that is what we must endure.

I find it almost unbearable that the USA Carnegie report on Education was entitled *Building Communities*[20] and that the new educational campaign *America 2000* acknowledges and pursues so many of the approaches I have mentioned while we in Britain have adopted a narrower and narrowing philosophy. The isolated, competitive, inward-looking school dislocated from its community by the random action of the market in parental choice is not the vibrant educational organism we need for the 1990s. Indeed it is no organism at all and that is the problem; it belongs to the mechanistic ideas of Adam Smith and the eighteenth century, not the ecological interdependence of individuals and systems which is the bright and guiding insight of the late twentieth century.

I conclude like this. The Great Debate and the reconnection of education with the world 'outside' was a necessary and valuable process. But the atomization of our system will not serve our economic, social or spiritual needs. If these forces remain dominant then teachers and their collaborators will have to keep the spirit of human kindness and vision of nobility alive in the catacombs while rendering unto Caesar the things that are Caesar's. But my fervent hope is that we can come to our senses in time and realize that, properly resourced and encouraged, our schools can do all the instrumental things asked of them and much more besides. And that much more will be far more important in the Britain of the future.

NOTES

1.   DES (1985) *Better Schools*, White Paper. London: HMSO.
2.   Sacks, J. (1990) 'The Reith Lectures for 1990', *The Listener*, 6 December 1990, p. 17.
3.   Drucker, P. (1989) *The New Realities*. London: Heinemann.
4.   Resnick, L.B. (1989) 'Cognitive Apprenticeships' in Resnick, L.B. (ed.) *Knowing, Learning and Instruction: Essays in Honor of Robert Glaser*. Hillsdale, NJ: Lawrence Erlbaum.
5.   Zuboff, S. (1988) *The Age of the Smart Machine: The Future of Work and Power*. New York: Basic Books.

6. Institute of Manpower Studies (1984) *Competence and Competition: Training and Education in the Federal Republic of Germany, the United States and Japan*. London: NEDO.
7. Tomlinson, J. (1986) 'Public Education, Public Good', *Oxford Review of Education*, 12 (3).
8. Marshall, C. (1991) 'Culture Change', *RSA Journal*, CXXXIX/5414, 1991.
9. Halsey, A.H. (1972) *Educational Priority*. London: HMSO.
10. Cox, C.B. and Dyson, A.E. (1971) *The Black Papers on Education*. London: Davis-Poynter; originally published, London: Critical Quarterly Society, 1969.
11. OECD (1975) *Educational Development Strategy in England and Wales*. Paris: OECD.
12. See note 1.
13. See RSA (1991) *Education for Capability: The Campaign*. London: Royal Society of Arts.
14. See DES/HMI (1977) *Curriculum 11-16: Working Papers by HM Inspectorate. A Contribution to Current Debate*. London: HMSO.
    DES/HMI (1981) *Curriculum 11-16: A Review of Progress*. London: HMSO.
    DES/HMI (1983) *Curriculum 11-16: Towards a Statement of Entitlement. Curricular Reappraisal in Action*. London: HMSO.
15. DES/HMI (1985) *The Curriculum from 5 to 16*. London: HMSO.
16. Miliband, D. (1991) *Markets, Politics and Education: Beyond the Education Reform Act*. London: Institute for Public Policy Research.
17. Neave, G. (1988) 'Education and Social Policy: Demise of an Ethic or Change of Values ?', *Oxford Review of Education*, 14(3).
18. Hurd, D. (1988) *The New Statesman*, 27 April 1988.
19. Hollis, M. (1988) 'Atomic Energy and Moral Glue'. Unpublished paper given at a conference, *The Philosopher's Eye*, organized by Cheshire LEA, Warwick University Institute of Education and The Royal Institute of Philosophy, 15 October 1988.
20. Commission on Future of Community College Staff (1988) *Building Communities: A Vision for a New Century*. Washington: American Association of Community & Junior Colleges.

Chapter 6

Liberal Education and Vocational Preparation

Richard Pring

The Ruskin College lecture of Lord Callaghan was a landmark in the development of education in the last few decades. Indeed one could say that most that has happened since 1978 has been a kind of footnote to Ruskin—just as most of philosophy might be seen as a footnote to Plato. Lord Callaghan questioned the standards which prevailed in our schools, but also the relevance of the curriculum to the needs of a society which had to survive in a tough and competitive economic world. Particularly there needed to be a greater emphasis upon the technological and the vocational relevance of schooling.

Since the Ruskin speech there have been many initiatives which have aimed at meeting these criticisms and I shall be referring to them. But beneath the practical details of new courses and changed curriculum are deeper issues about the very aims of education—the purposes which schools should serve and the values which they should embody. It is that aspect of the debate that this paper will focus upon. But I wish first to set the scene—to outline as briefly as possible the problems to be faced and the solutions being offered. In pursuit of that I shall do the following:

—identify the criticisms which the education system post-Ruskin is a response to;

—delineate the confusing arrangements emerging to meet those criticisms;

—identify the deeper, more philosophical questions that need to be addressed concerning the aims of education.

CRITICISMS

There have been four main criticisms of the educational system.

(i) Standards

It is frequently stated, and sometimes argued, that standards are low and getting lower—both in absolute terms and in comparison with those of countries, such as Germany and Japan, with which we have to compete economically. Such a criticism has of course been with us for a long time, and it is difficult to see how standards could have been declining steadily for a hundred years or more. But the truth of these assertions is not easy to determine. It all depends on what you believe the aims of education to be ('standard' depends logically on aims and on the values implicit within those aims). It depends, too, on what counts as evidence to back up these claims (the number of GCSE passes, the increased staying on rate, the improved technological literacy?). And it depends also on who you think is most trustworthy in commenting upon the state of education (HMI or, for example, the Centre for Policy Studies?). But the truth or otherwise of these allegations is less important for my purposes than the effect that they have upon perceptions of the educational service and thus upon the changes which have taken place.

It should be noted that there is concern about standards in two very different ways. First, there is concern for the standards of literacy and numeracy amongst the majority. Hence, the back-to-basics movement and the criticism of what is seen to be the pupil-centred methods advocated by the Plowden Report. Secondly, however, there is concern over the betrayal of 'traditional learning' for the minority —the failure to maintain the curriculum and the teaching approaches that were typical of the grammar schools. Hence, the criticism of course work assessment rather than terminal written examinations; hence, too, the arguments for more grammar and for a return to a canon of English literature.

(ii)   Economic relevance

It is also claimed that what the pupils learn is not relevant to our economic needs, and this criticism is not aimed primarily at the standards of numeracy and literacy of the less able but at the attitudes, qualities and skills produced by traditional learning. What society needs, so it is argued, are people who are enterprising, who have the practical know-how to make a success of business, who see the economic significance of what they learn. Instead, traditional learning has engendered a disdain for the practical and for the economically relevant, indeed for the industrial base of our educational provision. The purer, the more abstract, the more theoretical, the less practical the subject, the greater its status.

It is, therefore, argued that the curriculum for all should become much more economically relevant—both the subjects taught and the way in which they are taught. Technology, far from being a subject for the less able, should be taken by all and indeed should permeate the curriculum. The whole learning experience should encourage the spirit of enterprise, not the contempt for the commercial virtues which too often is the case. The school should help the student find the appropriate vocational route, not leave it to chance.

It should be noted, however, that this criticism is not altogether compatible with the first one and indeed comes from different sources. The supporters of 'traditional learning' are not as keen as the employers on economic relevance or on fostering the virtues of enterprise and entrepreneurship. And these differences are reflected in the emerging educational arrangements.

(iii)   Personal relevance

The third area of criticism concerns the lack of motivation in many young people, reflected in the poor staying-on rates post-16. It is argued by some that a curriculum that has changed little in the development of the comprehensive system of education will not motivate those who need much more practical and vocationally relevant assignments. A 'grammar school for all' may have sounded attractive to parents in the 1960s; it seemed less attractive to their offspring. Therefore, so it is argued, a lot needs to be done to win back disillusioned pupils and to engage them once again in the enterprise of education—to persuade them that it is not only worthwhile in itself but also useful and materially rewarding.

(iv)   Social relevance

There are criticisms of the social product of our schools. Obviously there are anxieties about drug taking, about juvenile crime, about anti-social behaviour of various kinds. Sometimes, quite unjustifiably, schools are blamed for these ills, as though they can be held responsible for the influences of society in general. More positively, however, the schools are seen as forces for good in countering them. Therefore, schools have lessons in health education and social studies; they become the instruments for anti-drugs campaigns; and more recently they have been expected to promote citizenship.

Therefore, there has been, since Ruskin, a continuation of the criticisms made then— criticisms of falling standards, of economic irrelevance, of pupil dissatisfaction and of social failure. Many of these criticisms may be ill-judged, many lacking evidence. But that is not the point. If those criticisms are believed, then reforms to the educational system will be a response to those criticisms. And those reforms will be as relevant, as confused, as effective as the criticisms themselves.

CHANGING ARRANGEMENTS

There have been many developments in the last decade to meet these criticisms, although they hardly hang together in a coherent system.

(i)   Curriculum

The major attempt to address the problem of low standards is the provision of a National Curriculum together with the assessment of all pupils at four different stages. The National Curriculum is a reassertion of 'traditional learning', the identification of core and foundation subjects together with attainment targets which are drawn from the working parties' understanding of the key concepts, skills, facts or principles of the different subjects. The A-Level examinations have remained relatively unaffected by reforms because these are seen as 'the gold standard', the 'jewel in the crown', the 'flagship' of the educational system. There have also been reforms of the 16+ examinations with the GCSE stressing more practical modes of learning and encouraging assessment of course work. But the uneasy fit between the GCSE reforms, the assessments for the National Curriculum and the unreformed A-Level examinations has caused questioning of the standards implicit in the GCSE. There will be less importance attached to course work and practical assignments.

On the other hand there are many who wish to remain in education post-16 but for whom the A-Level examinations are clearly unsuitable. Indeed, it ought to be a matter of some concern to those who are trying to meet the criticisms referred to above that so many able people who embark upon A-Level courses either fail or drop out during the course (roughly 30 per cent in any one subject). In the last few years there has been a growth of prevocational courses which continue with the principle of general education but which add a vocational orientation. However, the conception of general education is very different from that embodied within the the subject-based curriculum of GCSE and A-Level.

The prevocational curriculum (represented by such innovations as the Certificate of Prevocational Education or the BTEC First Certificate) starts from questioning the kinds of qualities, mental capacities, skills, understandings that young people need in order to live satisfactory lives. And 'satisfactory' includes meeting their own professional needs as well as the economic needs of the society in which they are to work. Thus, there is an emphasis upon communication skills, numeracy, the acquisition of defensible values which will sustain them when life gets tough, self-knowledge in relation to career choices, skills in using information technology, social and economic awareness of the context in which they live and work. There is an emphasis upon practical 'know-how' as much as upon propositional 'know-that'. Although much of the prevocational development took place in further education, it percolated down to the schools, and indeed entered into them particularly through the introduction of the Technical and Vocational Initiative (TVEI) into schools after 1982.

Nonetheless, the quite separate vocational training remained as a strong tradition after 16— in the workplace and in colleges of further education (CFE). 'Vocational Courses' are characterized by precise learning objectives related to specific employment requirements—the skills and knowledge required of a plumber, say. Generally speaking, such courses have not used the vocational objectives as a vehicle for delivering more generally educational qualities and understandings.

The changing curriculum, therefore, in response to the criticisms outlined above, maintains three quite distinctive traditions, especially in the post-16 phase of non-compulsory education and training, but increasingly, too, during the compulsory phase. What is referred to as the 'academic curriculum' maintains the education that was typical of the grammar school—an aggregate of subjects representing major disciplines of knowledge with an emphasis upon traditional modes of learning. Although there have been innovations through GCSE, with increased emphasis upon course work, such changes are being questioned as an erosion of standards. At the same time, fitting uneasily with the academic tradition has been the attempt to introduce more student-centred learning through TVEI—challenging prevailing teaching styles, challenging, too, prevailing conceptions of 'standards', as such innovations stress the process of learning. After 16, there are more job-related courses, often taken part-time in association with the workplace—a vocational curriculum only marginally affected by considerations of general education. However, there are suggestions that such vocationalism should enter the schools much earlier for those young people who are failed by the academic tradition—equipping them more effectively for the world of work.

(ii)   Qualifications

There is a changing pattern of assessments and qualifications to match these different curriculum traditions. Clearly the National Curriculum is assessed through the many attainment targets of the foundation subjects at key stages 1 to 4. Every pupil's attainment in the range of subjects which constitutes a balanced education will then be quantified and labelled. Comparisons can then be made between pupil and pupil, or between one pupil's performance at different stages of his or her schooling, or between schools as each aggregates the total scores of its pupils. The 16+ examinations (GCSEs) remain and will eventually be made to reflect performance on the national assessments at key stage 4. The normal progression for successful GCSE pupils will be into the narrower, more concentrated AS- or A-Level courses which provide the matriculation requirements for the university.

However, there is now a growing choice of qualifications both during the compulsory period of schooling and subsequently. The CGLI are offering a Diploma in Vocational Education which can be offered at three levels—Foundation, Intermediate, and National. This will replace CPVE. It embraces the prevocational approach to the curriculum referred to above, and it offers a route (so it is claimed) into higher education. It provides a very flexible framework, such that the Diploma student might also study for an A-Level. Meanwhile, BTEC continues to offer its First Certificate, leading on to the Ordinary and the Higher National Diplomas. These once again stress coherence and educational breadth through vocational relevance. And, as with the CGLI, they reach down into the schools, encouraging vocational options to parts of the National Curriculum.

Meanwhile, efforts are being made to make sense out of the enormous jungle of vocational qualifications. The National Vocational Qualification is offered at four different levels, bringing a common vocabulary to statements of competence in plumbing or engineering or commerce. The specific competences required by a particular job are agreed by the relevant professional and industrial bodies. The aim is to have a comprehensive list of competences, and an assessment system to match, that will cover the whole of industry and commerce.

There do, of course, remain many other bodies which offer vocational and prevocational qualifications—particularly, the Royal Society of Arts (RSA) which for many years have provided qualifications in commercial skills and knowledge and in design and the arts. But the purpose of this very brief account is to show the range of qualfications, often in competition with each other, which are awarded for achievement within the academic, prevocational and vocational courses in school and college. To what extent do these meet the criticisms outlined above? Or to what extent do they get in the way of a coherent system of education and training which should aim at a broadly based but vocationally relevant route through school into further training, higher education, and employment?

(iii)   Institutions

Not only are we seeing innovations in curriculum and qualifications, but the institutional arrangements within which these innovations are to take place are themselves changing. The National Curriculum Council (NCC) and the Curriculum Council for Wales (CCW) oversee the developments within the National Curriculum—the attainment targets and programmes of study at different levels, as well as the guidelines on cross-curricular dimensions, themes and skills. The Schools Examinations and Assessment Council (SEAC) both develops the assessments for the National Curriculum, and advises the Secretary of State on approval of examinations. Seeking the approval of SEAC are the GCSE and A-Level examination boards with the massive range of overlapping syllabuses from which schools might choose. Earlier attempts by SEAC to reduce the number of syllabuses offered at A-Level have been shelved. But there are, too, the vocational examination boards—BTEC, CGLI, RSA and others—which are providing qualifications and, where those are offered within the compulsory period of schooling, seeking the approval of the Secretary of State. Meanwhile, the National Council for Vocational Qualifications (NCVQ) is seeking to provide some simplification of the vocational qualifications and equivalences between these and the non-vocational ones.

However, the institutional world of examination and assessment is not the only complication in the search for coherence. There are many other voices in the debate on the welfare of education and training. Higher education sets matriculation requirements for entry and in the past these have in effect influenced the kind of qualifications that schools might sensibly offer. Employers, represented by the Confederation for British Industry (CBI), say what the outcomes of education and training should be, and therefore the newly formed Training and Enterprise Councils (TECs) will not only be responsible for ensuring the provision of adult and youth training programmes but also will exercise influence over the vocational relevance of the school curriculum. Local education authorities (LEAs) have a diminishing role in the inspection of courses and in co-ordinating local education and training provision, as colleges of FE and sixth form colleges assume corporate status and schools are encouraged to opt out. Three government departments have, quite independently, intervened in the curriculum of schools and colleges—the Department of Employment (DE) and the Department of Trade and Industry (DTI) as well as the DES. The DE funding of TVEI was the largest government sponsorship ever of curriculum change prior to the National Curriculum.

This all too brief summary does however reflect a change in the organization of the provision of education which is quite massive in scale—and unpredictable in its consequences. It reflects a particular set of beliefs, largely unco-ordinated, about the criticisms referred to and about the possible solutions. These are: first, that there is a need for central control and specification of national standards (hence, the National Curriculum, the standard assessments, the subjection of examining boards to SEAC scrutiny, the national vocational qualifications); second, however, that competition and indeed market forces must rule within this framework (hence, the gradual dissolution of LEA power and the establishment of locally managed schools and colleges; hence, too, the gradual growth of a voucher and credit system in youth training, reflecting the view that money must follow students and trainees as they seek out quality and relevance); third, employers must be significant partners in the whole enterprise (hence, the establishment of TECs and the role of employers on governing bodies of schools and colleges).

The system does, however, remain unco-ordinated, and it is doubtful whether the changes as described will meet the criticisms. There are many reasons for this: the increasing fragmentation of a system at a time when co-ordination and coherent planning are needed; the competition between examining boards when a much more straightforward set of routes through education and training into higher education and employment is required; the rather arbitrarily created and allocated grants from different government departments replacing guaranteed block grants, thereby jeopardizing continuity and long-term planning; the elimination of a layer of expertise at local government level which removes a much needed advisory and administrative service; the unco-ordinated empowering of employers in a service which is responsible for much wider and long-term educational goals. But above all, these changes do not address the deep-down division between the academic and the vocational, between liberal learning and job-related preparation, which is built in to the institutional divisions and the separate academic, prevocational and vocational routes, demanding such early and often arbitrary choices from young people.

The government has made an attempt to pull together these different strands of academic learning and professional training—but has in fact left things as they are. First, 'core skills' (a concept developed within the prevocational courses) were proposed as elements to be incorporated within the A-Level syllabuses. Such a vocationally relevant core included communication skills, numeracy, problem-solving skills, personal effectiveness and facility in using information technology. Recently arrived virtues such as enterprise and entrepreneurship should permeate the so-called academic curriculum. However, reform of A- or AS-Level seems to have been shelved, and 'core skills' are not at the top of the agenda. Second, encouragement was given to a 'common framework', with ease of transfer between vocational and academic qualifications, and NVQ (spelt out at level 2 in terms of equivalences with GCSE, at level 3 with a BTEC ordinary or two A-Levels at grade E). To help with this, a new Diploma was proposed which, at ordinary level, would be obtained for GCSEs and/or certain vocational qualifications, and, at advanced level, would be obtained for two A-Levels or a BTEC or NVQs at level 3. Two sets of certificates for the price of one seems a good bargain. But most people can recognize inflation when they see it. It does nothing to improve the value of what one is doing, or address the criticisms that have been outlined.

LIBERAL EDUCATION AND VOCATIONAL PREPARATION

One can tackle the problems that have been identified at different levels. At one level is the need to change the qualifications, to simplify them, to make connections so that students might see coherence and continuity in their studies through the different phases of education. Thus, A-Levels need to be reformed so that they are continuous with the more practical approaches in GCSE; they need to be broadened; they need to be connected (possibly through modular designs) with the more vocationally oriented BTEC.

At another level, the institutions need to be brought together again within a *system* of education—reversing the fragmentation that has occurred as schools seek grant-maintained status, as colleges of FE and sixth form colleges obtain corporate status outside the control of LEAs, and as money moves with students in a bidding process between private and public institutions.

However, at a deeper level are the more philosophical problems about the aims of education and training, about the idea of liberal education which enters into the academic tradition and the idea of vocational relevance which is embodied within the training programmes and the vocational qualifications obtained.

The distinction between academic and vocational studies is often regarded as self-evident and those who aspire to proceed to higher education generally pursue academic rather than vocational studies. In ensuring continuity between school and higher education, the National Curriculum aimed to provide entitlement to a broadly based academic curriculum for all. However, it has subsequently been argued by the Secretary of State that such a curriculum is to be curtailed so that vocational elements might, where necessary, be included. Furthermore, after the end of compulsory schooling, choices are available between the academic routes into higher education (A-Level) and the vocational routes into higher education or employment (BTEC and CGLI—all equated with levels of NVQ).

There are two ways in which this division is being challenged. The first concerns the inappropriateness of either a narrowly academic or a narrowly vocational education. It is argued by employers that economic performance is affected, on the one hand, by the lack of industrial and commercial understanding, by the absence of such economically relevant qualities as 'entrepreneurship' and 'enterprise', and by the neglect of work-related skills amongst those whose education has focused (often rather narrowly) upon particular intellectual disciplines, and, on the other hand, by the narrow focus upon competence unenlightened by liberal learning amongst those who have been vocationally trained. Somehow (we are told) we need to vocationalize the academic and liberalize the vocational. How can physics be taught, to a high academic standard certainly, but with its relevance to industry or to environmental issues made more explicit? How might chemistry be taught in an intellectually respectable way through the engagement in practical tasks? How might the training of carpenters be so undertaken as to indicate the wider aesthetic and scientific context of the craft?

The second way in which the distinction between the vocational and the academic is challenged is more fundamental—namely, the very basis of the distinction. Thus, why is science or engineering regarded as academic rather than vocational? Where, in this division, lie such practical pursuits as music or art? Why is not the rigorous pursuit of the crafts (requiring intelligence, judgement, knowledge, understanding) regarded as academic?

Different arguments might be provided at this stage for the maintenance of the distinction (concerned with knowledge for its own sake rather than for relevance, with theoretical rather than with practical understanding, with thinking rather than with doing). But far too often these arguments remain tenuous—and indeed irrelevant to a shifting curriculum with redrawn lines of progress through to 18.

(i) The liberal ideal

There are, of course, many versions of the liberal ideal of education. But one which has had such a massive influence on the dominant mode of academic education has been that of Newman, for whom liberal education is simply the cultivation of the intellect as such and its object is nothing more or less than intellectual excellence.

Such liberal education was based firmly on the nature of knowledge, learnt not as a set of inert and discrete ideas but as disciplines of active thinking, internalized and interconnecting with each other. And this idea of liberal education has dominated the formation of our educational institutions at every level and the shape and content of the learning promoted by them.

A summary of the main features of this notion of liberal education would be as follows. First, what should be learnt is rooted firmly within intellectual disciplines. Secondly, to be educated is to be initiated into these disciplines—that is, to have grasped the basic concepts, acquired the essential skills, mastered the techniques of enquiry, developed the moral habits of these fundamental ways of knowing the world and of shaping experience (the historical, philosophical, scientific, aesthetic and poetic 'voices'). Thirdly, the point or the value of the apprenticeship into the intellectual traditions, through which we come to understand and to shape our experience, requires no further justification than reference to their own intrinsic value. The cultivation of the intellect or the participation in the conversation between generations is intrinsically worthwhile. Indeed, to answer the question 'Why is it worthwhile?' would, if seriously addressed, require participation in that very conversation. Fourthly, that initiation is a hard and a laborious task. It requires a time and a place set apart. It needs, in other words, schools and universities separated from the world of business and usefulness. Fifthly, the control and the direction of that conversation, and thus of the initiation into it, must lie in the hands of those who are authorities within it—certainly not government or industry or the community at large.

All this is reflected in an understanding of university and of school education which, if not universally agreed, was certainly dominant until recently. Universities, though funded mainly from central government, had no truck with external interference in what should be taught or in how students should be assessed. Research, too, was in the main determined by the research interests of the faculty and by the research problems arising from within the respective disciplines. Furthermore, what was selected for students to learn was determined not by subsequent usefulness but by that core of studies generally recognized by scholars to be central to an understanding of that discipline at this stage of its evolution. In that respect, the undergraduate programme might reflect the research interests of the department.

This intellectual autonomy of universities is reflected in the nature of the transaction between teacher and students in schools. Generally speaking, the secondary school curriculum had changed little since the 1904 regulations which divided it into roughly the same subject categories as those which typified the average university. Success in those subjects gave entry to those 'basic units' which, together, constituted the conversation within higher education. The curriculum was based on a particular selection from that culture—a selection from the current state of knowledge as that was reflected in university departments and thereby in the 18+ examinations on whose boards the university departments were represented. Government, employers and parents had no voice in what should be taught. Indeed, Sir David Eccles, when Minister of Education in the early 1960s, referred to the 'secret garden of the curriculum', a garden tended entirely by the professionals, where politicians dare not tread.

(ii)   The vocational alternative

Vocational education is a fairly elastic term and it covers many different ways in which the relationship between education and preparation for the world of work might be understood. But, whatever the distinctions to be made within 'vocational education', there are important differences between this general concept on the one hand and the liberal ideal on the other. There is a significant shift in the language through which the transaction between teacher and learner is to be understood—and one which philosophers of education have yet to address.

Vocational preparation signifies the acquisition of skills, qualities, attitudes and knowledge that are judged to be important for entry into the world of work—either because the economy needs them (trained engineers, say) or because the individual would otherwise be less able to make sense of that world and to make personal profit within it. It can be pitched at different levels of generality—from the encouragement of more young people to study science (because the economy needs more trained scientists) to the skewing of the science syllabus towards its industrial application, or from the promotion of highly generalized and transferable skills to the training in specific job-related competencies. But, whatever the level of generality, there is this in common, namely, the shaping of the transaction between teacher and learner by considerations other than those which are internal to the intellectual disciplines themselves. There is an undermining of the autonomy which previously belonged to the educational and academic communities.

One might make the following points about the more vocationally oriented curriculum. First, the value of the educational encounter between teacher and student lies partly in the external purposes which it serves—in particular the economic well-being either of the individual or of society generally. Secondly, therefore, the curriculum must be planned in terms of specific objectives which arise, not from within the intellectual disciplines themselves, but from an analysis of what the economy needs or what skills certain occupations demand—hence, the growing insistence upon clearly defined and easily measured competencies. Thirdly, the content of the curriculum, aimed at achieving these objectives, must be relevant to industry and commerce. Fourthly, the context of learning must be, as far as possible, in a realistic economic setting. Fifthly, the educational experience as a whole should foster attitudes and dispositions such as entrepreneurship and enterprise not normally associated with the more detached frame of mind of the liberally educated person. Sixthly, people from outside the academic and educational communities must be partners in the establishment of these objectives and in assessing whether or not they have been reached.

With this vocationalizing of education, certain features of the liberal ideal are being challenged to a degree that is not fully appreciated. There is an implicit disdain for the pursuit of knowledge for its own sake, for the engagement in that conversation between the generations of mankind which has no end beyond the engagement itself. And no longer are the guardians of standards the authoritative voices within that conversation. For those reasons the distinctive forms of knowledge, which, in the competing accounts of liberal education, determined the logical structure of the process of learning, no longer provide the prime sources upon which the teacher should draw in the cultivation of the intellect. Instead, these sources are also externally agreed competencies, disconnected from the world of ideas which is the central concern of liberal education. Personal development becomes personal effectiveness; understanding and appreciation give way to skills and competences; the *process* of learning becomes subservient to the measurable *product*. Indeed, the gaining of qualifications—NVQ, for example—may require no course, no transaction between teacher and learner, since what is learnt is logically disconnected from the process of learning. All that the candidate needs to do is to submit himself to the particular tests of competence.

(iii)　Reconciling the differences: the philosophical agenda

I have drawn a sharp contrast between the idea of liberal education and the idea of vocational preparation as they vie with each other for dominion over the curriculum of school and of higher education. Perhaps the contrast is too sharp; in reality there are reconciliations and compromises. But these compromises are not easy. The 'vocationalizing' and the 'economizing' of the language through which education is described and evaluated (with its audits, performance indicators, cost-effectiveness of curriculum delivery, quality assurance, competency-based objectives, value addedness, inputs and outputs, usefulness) transforms our understanding of educational activities and of the values attributed to them. And the problems of compromise have resulted in the determination to create different routes—the traditional educational one for some and the vocational one for the many.

There is a need to re-assess the idea of liberal education in the light of this vocational challenge. To what extent are the criticisms valid? And how far does meeting the criticisms require a re-examination of those features of the liberal concept which seem most at odds with the idea of vocational preparation—namely, the aims and values to be pursued, the structure and content of the knowledge to be acquired, and the respective virtues and dispositions to be fostered?

In reality, two courses of action are available in the reconstitution of the educational system. The first is to recognize the differences and to make available two distinct routes, the educational and the vocational. The second course of action is to re-examine the liberal ideal, and to see how far it can be made vocationally relevant without the educational ideal being jeopardized. And that, surely the only solution, we have hardly begun to address.

Chapter 7

Beyond Ruskin:
Recent Conceptions of Children's Learning and Implications for Primary School Practice

Neville Bennett

I was pleased to accept the invitation to participate in this series of lectures because, like Lord Callaghan, I was heavily involved in the controversies which characterized the educational context in 1976. In April of that year we published a book entitled *Teaching Styles and Pupil Progress*.[1] Its conclusions were that achievement in the '3 Rs' tended to be higher in so-called formal classrooms; that it mattered how much time teachers devoted to the '3 Rs', how involved their pupils were, and how they structured their curriculum. It also concluded that informal teaching could be effective, but only in the hands of teachers with high levels of organization and skill.

Such findings were not particularly new. They accorded with the findings of other studies both in Britain and the United States, and indeed with virtually every study done on this topic since then. But at that time they challenged a powerful orthodoxy, an orthodoxy reflected in, and sustained by, the influential Plowden Report.[2] In 1976 that orthodoxy was already under fire, fuelled mainly by the notorious William Tyndale affair, the closure of a progressive primary school at the insistence of its working-class parents and governors. Levels of public anxiety had also been raised by the spectre of falling standards, an issue which was being addressed by rhetoric rather that by evidence, and capitalized on by yet another Black Paper.[3] The publication of our book unwittingly gave the educational right the findings they had been waiting for. The educational climate was thus ripe for controversy, a controversy captured by the clichés of the popular press.

It is of interest to learn, in this context, that Lord Callaghan himself reports being warned off—to keep off the educational grass. He referred to this in his Ruskin speech. 'Some people', he suggested, 'would wish that the subject-matter and purpose of education should not have public attention focused on it; nor that profane hands should be allowed to touch it.' I too experienced such reproof from the ideologues of the day, and other sundry nasties. How dare I question practices which were self-evidently right. Had not they done their own cardiac evaluations? They knew in their hearts it was true! How dare I come up with the wrong answer? Messianic zeal was the order in those heady days. Not much has changed in this regard. The ideologues of the romantic liberal left have simply been replaced by the ideologues of the market-oriented right.

But enough of 1976. What has happened to primary education in the meantime? What are the current priorities, and what of the future?

Lord Callaghan could not have envisaged the waves of innovation and change which have swept over our schools since his Ruskin speech, most of which have been imposed from without. A new National Curriculum, new and ever-changing assessment and recording procedures, local management of schools, new governing bodes, an increasingly weakened LEA structure, a Parents' Charter—the list is almost endless. Now all those must have had far-reaching effects on the way we teach primary children you might think. Well, if they have, they are not easy to see. If you read the substantial research effort on primary practice over the last fifteen years, and combine these findings with the ever-increasing number of HMI reports, it is clear that the same issues predominate, the same strengths and the same weaknesses prevail. The waves of structural change appear to have washed over classroom practice.

At one level, of course, we should be congratulating teachers for resisting the political winds of change. It was not so long ago that teachers were constantly being criticized for taking on one fad after another. On the other hand it is a little worrying that practice is so hard to shift, particularly when there seem to be good grounds for doing so.

Over the last decade or so educational and psychological research, often grounded in the classroom, has extended our understanding of teaching and learning and pointed up important implications for improving the quality of classroom practice. In the remainder of this paper I want to consider two areas which, I believe, have particular significance for primary teaching—our changing conceptions of how children learn, and the influence on learning of teacher knowledge.

HOW CHILDREN LEARN

Recent research and theorizing about cognitive development views learning as an active, constructive, intellectual process that occurs gradually over a period of time. It is not simply an additive process. Knowledge cannot, to use a common metaphor, be poured into learners' heads with the hope that learning will automatically occur or accumulate. Understandings of new knowledge can only take place, or be constructed in the minds of individual learners, through a process of making sense of that new knowledge in the light of what they already know. In other words, learning is a process of constructing new knowledge on the basis of current knowledge. Therefore, what children learn in classrooms will depend to a large extent on what they already know. Children, of whatever age, enter the classroom with extensive, but divergent levels of prior knowledge and conceptions which they have acquired from the myriad of everyday influences and experiences—books, TV, talking to parents and friends, visits to places of interest, previous learning in school and so on. Consequently, they are likely to have some knowledge, some conceptions, of whatever learning topics they are confronted with in the classroom.

However, these conceptions, or schemata, are likely to be incomplete, hazy or even plain wrong. They are, nevertheless, the children's current ideas, which they use to make sense of everyday experiences. In other words, children do not come to any lesson empty-headed; they come with partial schemata. The teacher's job, then, is to find effective ways for children to modify, extend or elaborate their schemata. Indeed we can define learning in these terms—the extension, modification or elaboration of existing cognitive schemata.

That children in the same class have very different schemata is now well recorded, particularly in relation to concepts in maths and science. For example, a local teacher of 9-year-olds recently ascertained her children's schema of shadows.[4] One third argued that a shadow is an area blotted out from the sun's rays by an object, whereas another third said that a shadow is caused by the body acting as a mirror which reflects the sun's rays on to the floor. One child believed that a shadow is a little black thing that follows you around!

That children have misconceptions is not limited to the primary school; it happens throughout the education system, indeed throughout the world. A Swedish research group,[5] for example, considered the conceptions of 12- to 15-year-olds about light and its propagation. They asked the pupils to explain how you can see a book—what happens between the eyes and the book.

Of 600 students who answered this, only 20 per cent showed signs of having understood that light is something which exists and propagates, a key image to understand optics. Fifty per cent of students thought that visual rays, looks or impulses were actually emitted by the eye.

Such research into children's conceptions has shown that they often hold unorthodox views about a wide range of topics taught in school; that these conceptions shape how they make sense of new information, thereby often exacerbating learning difficulties; and that they often find it difficult to modify their conceptions, particularly in areas like science, where they prefer to hold onto their intuitive ideas.

So, in the classroom, children have schemata which are differentially complete or correct, some of which are idiosyncratic and others which are shared. They make sense of new inputs by constructing links with their prior knowledge. It is assumed that the construction of these links is an intellectual process involving the generation, checking and restructuring of ideas in the light of those already held. This construction of meaning is a continuous and active intellectual process. Not surprisingly, this view of learning is often referred to as 'constructivist'.

There is little argument amongst theorists that learning involves the construction of knowledge through experience. Arguments occur in relation to the conditions under which such learning is optimized—should learning be individual or social? This argument is captured well by Jerome Bruner[6] in his contrast of children as 'social beings' and 'lone scientists'.

A quiet revolution has taken place in developmental psychology in the last decade. It is not only that we have begun to think again of the child as a social being—one who plays and talks with others, learns through interactions with parents and teachers—but because we have come once more to appreciate that through social life, the child acquires a framework for integrating experience, and learning how to negotiate meaning in a manner congruent with the requirements of the culture. 'Making sense' is a social process; it is an activity that is always situated within a cultural and historical context.

Before that, we had fallen into the habit of thinking of the child as an 'active scientist', constructing hypotheses about the world, reflecting upon experience, interacting with the physical environment and formulating increasingly complex structures of thought. But this active, constructing child had been conceived as a rather isolated being, working alone at her problem-solving. Increasingly we see now that, given an appropriate, shared social context, the child seems more competent as an intelligent social operator than she is a 'lone scientist' coping with a world of unknowns.

This support for the child as a social being rather than a lone scientist constitutes an attack on the Piagetian view of learning, the view accepted unreservedly by the Plowden Report, which assumes that intellectual competence is a manifestation of a child's largely unassisted activities. Indeed it was this view which spawned the ideology of the individualization of learning, to which I will return later.

The conception of the learner as a social being stresses far more the importance of the social setting in learning, and emphasizes in particular the role of negotiating and sharing in the classroom. As one theorist[7] argued, 'Learning awakens a variety of internal developmental processes that are able to operate only when the child is interacting with people in his environment and in co-operation with his peers.' Social interaction is assigned a central role in facilitating learning. Thus a child's potential for learning is revealed, and indeed is often realized, in interactions with more knowledgeable others. These 'more knowledgeable others' can be anybody—peers, siblings, the teacher, parents, grandparents and so on.

The basic idea is that children should be given work that is slightly too difficult, but that initially this is done with the cooperation of more knowledgeable others. Understanding gained cooperatively can then be used individually, or, as Vygotsky[8] put it, 'What a child can do today in cooperation, tomorrow he will be able to on his own.' It is now commonly agreed that the foundation of learning and development is cooperatively achieved success, and the basis of that success is language and communication. In other words, talk drives learning.

The belief that talk is central to learning is not new. The Bullock Report[9] devoted itself entirely to language, and welcomed the growth in interest in oral language: 'For we cannot emphasize too strongly our conviction of its importance in the education of the child.' It argued that all schools ought to have, as a priority objective, a commitment to the speech needs of their pupils.

The status of talk in the classroom was reinforced in the 1980s through the focus on oracy by the Assessment of Performance Unit (APU) which concluded that 'Pupils' performances could be substantially improved if they were given regular opportunities in the classroom to use their speaking and listening skills over a range of purposes, in a relaxed atmosphere.'[10]

Following this, the authors of the English National Curriculum recommended a separate language component for speaking and listening, thus demonstrating their belief in oracy. 'Our inclusion of speaking and listening as a separate profile component in our recommendations is a reflection of our conviction that these skills are of central importance to children's development.'[11]

To sum up, learning is now believed to be optimized in settings where social interaction, particularly between a learner and more knowledgeable others, is encouraged, and where cooperatively achieved success is a major aim. The medium for this success is talk, which is now widely accepted as a means to promoting pupils' understandings, and of evaluating their progress.

The implications of this conception of learners for classroom practice are considerable, and in opposition to one enduring facet of primary teaching. One constant element of teacher behaviour in my twenty-one years' experience of observing in classrooms, has been the sight of teachers running themselves ragged attempting to individualize teaching and learning to more than 30 children. And the fact is it has never worked properly. Although prescribing individualized learning, even the Plowden Report recognized that teachers could not be expected to operate such a system. Yet individual work has become a way of life for British primary school children. There has, however, been considerable concern among educationalists that this approach has serious problems associated with it.

The so-called Oracle study,[12] for example, argued that, 'The Plowden prescripts stressing discovery learning and the probing, questioning character of the teacher's role appear, at least with present class sizes, impossible of achievement.'

They considered the problem to be so serious that they recommended that 'total individualization must be ruled out as an option'. The problems of individualization reach a peak in the teaching of reading. Vera Southgate Booth[13] spelt this out in the early 1980s as follows:

> The pattern of the typical oral reading lesson would seem to indicate that teachers have been persuaded by educationists, and perhaps by reading experts, into thinking that individual help is

always best. Teachers would do well to question whether individual tuition is always necessary or always the most profitable use of their time, particularly when the contacts are as short as 30 seconds. Are there never groups of children, or occasionally a whole class, ready for the same piece of teaching or learning experience at the same time? If so, would not 10 or 15 minutes spent with a group occasionally be a more valuable use of the teacher's time?

In our own work[14] on the quality of pupil learning experiences we found exactly the same problem, and diagnosed it as a problem of organization.

As the actual time spent on reading and writing tuition is limited teachers should be experimenting with procedures by which this precious commodity—their own time—will be most profitably spent, to ensure that as much learning as possible is taking place. If a teacher were not driving herself so hard, for example by trying to give individual attention to 32 children in 20 minutes, she could experiment with methods or organisation which might result in a more profitable use of the children's time so that they learned more, practised more and used their developing skills more.

This view was also echoed by HMI.[15]

Where children were given too little help in organising their work the quality of what was done suffered to some extent because many worked too often as individuals rather than as members of a group or class. Individual work, when overdone, allows the teacher little time to discuss difficulties with the children in more than a superficial way and provides too few opportunities for the children to learn from each other.

Sufficient has been said, I think, to point up that total individualization is not a sensible policy for teacher or taught.

The major implication for teachers is thus for the structuring of classroom environments which offer the best opportunity for pupils to be involved in the social and cognitive activities entailed in building knowledge and understanding. This requires the translation of beliefs about pupils as 'social beings' into modes of classroom organization which encourage talk within cooperative endeavours. For many teachers this will involve shifts in teaching and management strategies.

However, let me be clear lest I be misunderstood. I am not calling for the abandonment of individual, or even whole-class, work. What is required is a change in balance toward more cooperative grouping, particularly in tasks demanding problem solving and knowledge application.

So what is new, you might say, 'I use groups'. Over the last few years we have devoted substantial amounts of our research effort to investigating classroom groups, and detailing, for teachers, how to implement 'real' cooperative groups effectively.[16] The sad fact is that although most teachers have children working *in* groups, very few teachers have children working *as* groups. Although most children sit next to other children for the great majority of their time, they work as individuals on their own individual tasks. Further, research on such groups by ourselves and others shows a pattern of poor quality talk, much of which is not related to the task. Little is cooperative in nature and much is gender determined, i.e. the great majority of talk is between pupils of the same sex, even in mixed groups. In short these are not contexts in which effective learning takes place.

Research on cooperative groups on the other hand shows that, when properly implemented, the amount of task-related talk increases substantially, cooperation is very high, learning improves and so does social development in the form of enhanced self-esteem and decreased ethnic prejudice and stereotyping.

HMI too have observed the improvements that cooperative group work can bring, arguing in their mathematics report,[17] for example, that 'Cooperative work was a strong and distinctive feature of the best mathematics seen, with pupils seeking together a solution to an intellectual or practical problem.'

I do not believe that primary teachers do not appreciate or understand the importance of talk. It may simply be that the link between talk and grouping has not previously been made explicit, or it may be that grouping has emerged, as one commentator argued, as an organizational device rather than as a means of promoting more effective learning, or perhaps exists for no reason other than fashion and ideology dictate it. Irrespective of the reason, the implementation of cooperative learning must be a priority in the future.

TEACHER KNOWLEDGE

The second area I wish to consider, teacher knowledge, links with the first. For learning to be effective i.e for children's schema to be extended and modified in developmentally appropriate ways, the teacher must first carefully diagnose the child's existing schema and identify any misconceptions apparent. Tasks then have to be planned through the transformation of programmes of study or statements of attainment into suitable classroom tasks, incorporating appropriate sequencing. These are then presented to the child or children with adequate and informative explanatory material. As the Select Committee on Achievement in Primary Schools[18] concluded, 'The skills of diagnosing learning success and difficulty, and selecting and presenting new tasks, are the essence of the teachers's profession, and vital to children's progress.'

However, this description of the teacher's role begs several questions. How can teachers transform content into effective learning tasks unless they have a thorough knowledge of that content? How can teachers know what counts for development or sequence in a subject area with which they are not thoroughly familiar? How can effective explanations be provided for children, incorporating appropriate analogies and metaphors, without subject-matter expertise? And how can teachers diagnose children's errors and misconceptions of concepts, such as the concept of force in science, if they themselves do not have that understanding?

There is an increasing body of research evidence which links subject matter knowledge to effective teaching and learning on both sides of the Atlantic, and our current work with student teachers supports this finding. There is also increasing evidence to show that teachers in training and experienced teachers, both primary and secondary, do not understand subjects in depth. It is not surprising, is it? In this country we train primary teachers as specialists in one or two areas of the curriculum and then expect them to be expert in nine or ten!

Nevertheless, concern about levels of teacher knowledge have increased through the 1980s. The DES, for example, in *Better Schools*[19] argued that the greatest obstacle to the continued improvement of science in primary schools is that many existing teachers lack a working knowledge of elementary science. This has been supported in a set of studies on primary teachers' understanding of science concepts.[20]

It was reported that the majority of teachers' views were based on a 'mixture of intuitive beliefs and half remembered textbook science from their school days, sometimes with incorrect or imprecise use of scientific language.' Another, smaller, group of teachers seemed not to possess any theoretical understanding of phenomena presented. This group had received little education in science at school and of necessity were able to explain the instances only at a perceptual level, or not at all. They concluded that the scientific thinking of many of the teachers studied resembled that of children, being limited to perceptual and observable entities.

Our own research in this area has taken us down two separate, but inter-related, paths. The first was to check out the levels of knowledge with which graduates entered Post-graduate Certificate of Education (PGCE) programmes. The implicit assumption on the part of government and its quangos such as the Council for the Accreditation of Teacher Education (CATE) is that they enter with sufficient knowledge to teach the National Curriculum. PGCE courses typically contain no explicit teaching of subject knowledge, nor are they required to. The second path led us to check with experienced teachers how competent they felt to teach the National Curriculum to levels 5 and 6 with their existing knowledge. Our aim here was to ascertain in-service priorities.[21, 22]

To test out the incoming knowledge of PGCE students we devised assessments based on the first 5 or 6 levels of the National Curriculum in Maths, Science and English, i.e. the limit to which most bright 11- or 12-year-olds might aspire. The questions in science were designed to represent the world of science which children would recognize, covering such things as the sequence of the life cycle of a horse chestnut, simple electric circuits and problems involving photosynthesis, gravity and force.

The average score was just 50 per cent. In general, their responses showed that they did not have a bank of concepts from which they can confidently apply their knowledge to make sense of everyday phenomena, and reveal the same kinds of misconceptions that children show. These students were tested again at the end of the course and, predictably perhaps, showed little change. Indeed comparison of their scores with a national group of able 11-year-olds showed that on average these children performed better on some items than the average student teachers.

There was a similar success rate in mathematics. Students were pretty good at things like number sequences but less good on percentages. When faced with the question, 'What is £18 as a percentage of £120?' only 6 in 10 got it right. They were least good on shapes and sub-sets of shapes. Overall, therefore, graduates entering PGCE courses do not have the knowledge necessary to teach to level 6 of the National Curriculum, and such knowledge is not currently explicitly taught. On the other hand it should be said that they learn a great deal about curriculum and pedagogy—despite what the Secretary of State, Mr Clarke, and some of his friends say.

So what of the present teaching force—how competent do they feel about teaching the National Curriculum with their present levels of knowledge? We have carried out two national surveys on this topic, one in 1989 and the latest in June of this year (1991), immediately after the Standard Assessment Task (SAT) assessment period. In both surveys we asked teachers to indicate in general their felt competence to teach each subject, and then in the core curriculum areas we asked them to react to individual statements of attainment. This was to give us a clearer idea of strengths and weaknesses within the subjects.

As Table 1 shows, in 1989 teachers felt most competent to teach English and mathematics. However, a third felt they could not handle science without substantial in-service input, and in music and technology they felt even less capable. In 1991 the general pattern did not change a great deal except that, in the intervening period, experience of teaching science appears to have given teachers some confidence in teaching it, and as a result it has climbed the rank order. At the same time, history and geography have declined, possibly a consequence of teacher reaction to the very extensive new programmes of study in these areas. Music and technology are still firmly anchored at the bottom.

To sum up, there is increasingly evidence to indicate that teacher knowledge is a vital ingredient in effective teaching. On the other hand the evidence shows that both teachers in

Table 1   Primary teachers' feelings of competence in teaching subjects of the National Curriculum

Percentage feeling competent with existing knowledge

1989 survey			1991 survey		
1	English	81	1	English	77
2	Maths	68	2	Maths	62
3	History	54	3	Science	41
4	Geography	48	4	Art	40
5	Art	48	5	History	38
6	PE	47	6	PE	37
7	RE	45	7	Geography	36
8	Science	34	8	RE	33
9	Music	27	9	Music	23
10	Technology	14	10	Technology	14

training, and experienced teachers, do not have sufficient grasp of the knowledge required to teach the necessary levels of the National Curriculum.

Some of the implications of these findings are obvious. Appropriate in-service training is a priority, but it needs to be training in depth, not the half- or full-day session that seems to be becoming typical under the new arrangements for local management of schools (LMS). Some implications are more difficult. For example, if subject matter knowledge were to be introduced into PGCE courses what would have to be left out in what is already an over-crowded course? And if training is to be more school-based in the future, where will the teaching of knowledge fit into this pattern? These are important questions for the future.

So where have we come since Ruskin? As a consequence of investigations of classroom practice, and the development of more adequate theory, our conceptions of children's learning in classrooms has changed, as Bennett and Carré[23] put it, from the Piagetian sandpit to the Vygotskian climbing frame, in which teachers and peers support, or scaffold, children's developing schemata through talk in a cooperative context. Our vision of the effective teacher has thus changed from that advocated in 1976. The teacher of the future will be knowledgeable in subject-matter, skilled at transferring content into worthwhile and appropriate tasks, able to set up management structures which maximize pupil talk in cooperative learning contexts, adept at providing the most adequate explanations and demonstrations, expert in the diagnosis of children's conceptions and misconceptions, and fluent in the provision of feedback and support to learners. Truly a paragon of pedagogical virtue, I hear you say! But, with the ideologues of the right calling for instruction rather than exploration, for more whole-class teaching, for streaming and wholesale specialist teaching in the junior school, our best hope for the future is the thinking professional primary teacher who will not be blown, hither and thither, by the ideologues of the day. We cannot return to the past, but we can improve on the present. As Martin Luther King nearly said—although we are not where we want to be; although we are not where we are going to be; thank goodness we are not where we were.

NOTES

1.   Bennett, N. (1976) *Teaching Styles and Pupil Progress*. London: Open Books.

2. Central Advisory Council for Education (England) (1969) *Children and their Primary Schools* (The Plowden Report). London: HMSO.
3. Cox, C.B. and Dyson, A. E. (eds.) (1975) *Black Paper 1975—The Fight for Education*. London: Dent.
4. Green, J.R. (1989) *Primary Children's Ideas in Science and Teaching Strategies to Develop Scientific Thinking*. M.Ed. dissertation, University of Exeter.
5. Anderson, B. and Karrquist, C. (1983) 'How Swedish pupils aged 12-15 years understand light and its properties', *European Journal of Science Education*, 5, pp. 387-402.
6. Bruner, J. and Haste, H. (1987) *Making Sense: The Child's Construction of the World*. London: Methuen.
7. Vygotsky, L.S. (1978) *Mind in Society: The Development of Higher Psychological Processes*. Cambridge, Mass.: Harvard University Press.
8. Vygotsky, L.S. (1962) *Thought and Language*. Cambridge, Mass.: MIT Press.
9. DES (1975) *A Language for Life* (The Bullock Report). London: HMSO.
10. Assessment of Performance Unit (1986) *Speaking and Listening*. Windsor: NFER/Nelson.
11. DES/WO (1989) *National Curriculum—English for Ages 5 to 11*. London/Cardiff: HMSO.
12. Galton, M., Simon, B. and Croll, P. (1980) *Inside the Primary Classroom*, London: Routledge & Kegan Paul.
13. Southgate, V., Arnold, H. and Johnson, S. (1981) *Extending Beginning Reading*. London: Heinemann.
14. Bennett, N., Desforges, C., Cockburn, A. and Wilkinson, B. (1984) *The Quality of Pupil Learning Experiences*. London: Erlbaum.
15. DES/HMI (1978) *Primary Education in England: A Survey by HMI*. London: HMSO.
16. See notes 12 and 14. Also Bennett, N. and Dunne, E. (1992) *Managing Classroom Groups*. Hemel Hempstead, Simon & Schuster.
17. DES/HMI (1989) *Aspects of Primary Education: The Teaching of Mathematics*. London: HMSO.
18. House of Commons (1986) *Achievement in Primary Schools*, Report of Select Committee on Education, Science and the Arts. London: HMSO.
19. DES (1985) *Better Schools*, White Paper. London: HMSO.
20. Kruger, C. and Summers, M. (1989) 'An investigation of some primary teachers' understandings of changes in materials', *School Science Review*, 71, pp. 17–27.
21. Wragg, E.C., Bennett, S.N. and Carré, C.G. (1989) 'Primary teachers and the National Curriculum', *Research Papers in Education*, 4, pp. 17-37.
22. Bennett, S.N., Wragg, E.C., Carré, C.G. and Carter, D.S.G. (1992) 'A longitudinal study of primary teachers' perceived competence in, and concerns about, National Curriculum implementation', *Research Papers in Education*, 6, (forthcoming).
23. Bennett, N. and Carré, C. (1993) *Learning to Teach*. London: Routledge.

Chapter 8

Meeting Special Educational Needs:
Towards the Year 2000 and Beyond
Peter Mittler

FAILING TO BENEFIT?

A fellow professor of education was asked during the course of a radio interview whether our education system had failed the children of this country. He replied that the system was very successful for the 15 per cent who reached higher education but less successful for the rest.

In the same vein, Eric Bolton, until recently Her Majesty's Senior Chief Inspector of Education, repeatedly emphasized in his annual 'state of the nation's education' review, that children of below average ability and attainments are badly served by our educational system and that 'the less academically able continue to suffer disproportionately from whatever chronic or acute problems affect the education service'.[1]

My concern here is with those children and young people who are not benefiting as well as they might from the education system, for whatever reason or combination of reasons. A small minority of these children would be regarded as having significant disabilities or handicaps, and some of them may be in special schools. But the vast majority are children in ordinary schools with limited or below average educational attainments, children who may or may not be described as having special educational needs but who are not benefiting from what schools have to offer.

These are not necessarily children of limited ability, and they cannot be characterized as underachievers, slow learners, low attainers, poorly motivated, as 'could do betters' or even as just plain lazy. These labels assume that the problems all lie within the child and ignore the possibility that the fault may also lie in part with the quality of schooling and teaching and the accessibility of the curriculum. Nor is it acceptable to blame the family. Comments such as 'What do you expect of a child from a home like that?' are as unacceptable as any racist or sexist stereotype. By the same token, it is futile to seek for single or simple causes for these difficulties. It is as inappropriate to put all the blame on schools for failing to help such pupils as it is to blame parents for failing to provide the kind of home environment conventionally associated with educational success.

These children are numerous—at one time it was common to refer to the 40 per cent of pupils who left schools without any recognized qualifications—but they cannot easily be defined and generalizations about their characteristics or needs are therefore bound to be misleading.

SOCIAL DISADVANTAGE AND POVERTY

Children who come from the poorer and more socially-disadvantaged section of our society are more at risk of educational underfunctioning and there is undoubtedly a link between poverty and educational attainment. This link is well documented but poorly understood. If poverty is defined in terms of families living on less than half the average income after housing costs have been met, official statistics indicate that 10 million people in the UK are now experiencing poverty, 4 million of them with young children in the family.

A recent report compiled for UNICEF by Professor Jonathan Bradshaw[2] showed that Britain had the sharpest rise in poverty of any European community country in the period 1975–1985. In that period, the number of children living in poverty in the UK rose from 1.6 to 3 million, a rise from 12 to 26 per cent. More than a third of the UK population was living in poverty or its margins in 1987, compared with slightly more than one in five in 1979, according to Professor Peter Townsend.[3]

The first casualty of poverty is the nutritional value of the child's diet which in turn affects general health as well as ability to benefit from schooling. The association between social class and health is very much better researched and has been the subject of many reports and recommendations, the most notable of which was the Black report by Sir Douglas Black, the then President of the Royal College of Physicians, Professor Peter Townsend and Dr Cyril Smith.[4] This report was virtually suppressed by the government and its recommendations dismissed as too costly. Although these links between poverty and health have been documented since the writings of Booth a century ago, the removal of milk and hot school dinners from many children makes one wonder whether the lessons have been learned.

SOCIAL BACKGROUND AND EDUCATIONAL OUTCOMES

Before they ever attend school at the age of five, there is already a marked gap between the cognitive and linguistic abilities of children from different social backgrounds. This is loosely attributed to an interaction of genetic and environmental influences which is itself poorly understood. Clearly, both are important: intelligence is to some extent genetically determined but environmental factors are also critical. Parents will always differ greatly in the kind of material, social and psychological environment which they provide for their children and in the kind of demands which they make of them. But these differences between families cut across all social classes; there are many children from poor homes who do well academically and professionally, just as there are children from middle-class families who are underachievers and unsuccessful. Children themselves contribute a powerful dynamic to this interaction; they are individuals in their own right not just the product of heredity and environment.

Once children begin to attend school, the gap in achievement between children of different social backgrounds tends to become wider rather than narrower. Of course, these are averages and trends, to which there are many exceptions but the research evidence is fairly consistent.

For the past 30 years, the National Child Development Study has been following the progress of all children born in the UK in a single week in March 1958. By the age of seven, five times as many children from social class five had reading problems as from social class one.[5] At 11, children with objective indicators of social disadvantage were more than seven times as likely to be sent to special schools than other children; at that time, social disadvantage was defined in terms of the presence of three indicators—low income qualifying for supplementary benefit, overcrowding (more than 1.5 persons per room) and being either in a single parent family or in one with more than five children.[6]

At 11, children from families where the father was in a non-manual occupation were three years more advanced in their reading and mathematics attainments, compared with children from social class five. At 16, three quarters of this latter group had below average reading and mathematics scores and a high proportion were reported as showing behaviour problems.[7]

At the age of 16 we find that, although the proportion of all pupils obtaining GCE Ordinary levels and latterly GCSE has shown a marked rise over the years, the gap between children of middle-class and working-class parents has not been significantly reduced.[8]

Turning to higher education, only 2 per cent of university graduates come from homes where the parents' occupation is semi-skilled or unskilled, compared with 17 per cent for the population as a whole and 29 per cent from professional families.

SCHOOL EFFECTIVENESS STUDIES

These differences in educational outcomes within British society have no simple or single explanation. In the past, the origins of educational failure or educational underfunctioning have been seen as lying almost entirely in the pupils themselves, in their families and in their social backgrounds. But in the past 10 to 15 years, we have looked increasingly at the characteristics of schools, how they are organized and managed, their social climate or ethos, and whether pupils are valued and treated with dignity. Searching questions have also been asked about the curriculum and the way in which it was taught, whether it was genuinely a curriculum for all or one designed largely for a small academically competent elite who will do well in exams and have no difficulty in entering higher education and the professions. School effectiveness studies typically study the progress of a large group of pupils over a period of years and relate these measures of progress over time to the characteristics and organisational style of the school.

The first major school effectiveness study was published as *Fifteen Thousand Hours* some 12 years ago by Professor Michael Rutter and his colleagues.[9] An equally influential study of London junior schools by Professor Peter Mortimore and his colleagues was published in 1988 under the significant title of *School Matters*.[10] These and other studies showed that schools drawing pupils from similar catchment areas differ very considerably in the results achieved by their pupils. Thus, two 7-year-old children from very similar backgrounds and with identical test scores and educational attainments can have totally different outcomes at 11, 14 and 16, depending on the school which they attend.

There is now a substantial body of research on what makes an effective school. One of the characteristics of such schools is that they cater fully for all their pupils, regardless of background, and make no prior assumptions about children's potential based on their background or home circumstances. It was this refusal to predict which made it possible for a girl with Down's syndrome not only to be accepted in a Cheshire secondary school but to be awarded six GCSE passes this summer.

CAN THE ACHIEVEMENT GAP BE NARROWED?

Although the gap in educational achievements between children from different social backgrounds is alarmingly large and indeed widens as pupils get older, there are schools that seem able to swim against the tide and to narrow the gap quite significantly. This at least was the finding reported by Professor Sally Tomlinson and Dr David Smith in their study of inner-city multi-racial comprehensive schools.[11] They showed that some schools are singularly more successful than others in helping children from the poorest and most disadvantaged backgrounds to increase their rate of progress and to improve on earlier poor educational performance. Unfortunately, the same cannot be said of all schools. For example, there is some evidence that the recently reported fall in reading standards in primary schools is closely related to socio-economic circumstances and is most marked in areas of poverty and disadvantage.

A special effort was made to address this problem in inner-city schools in Leeds, alongside problems arising from multi-cultural, multi-ethnic and gender-related needs. Four hundred extra teachers and 130 coordinators and other advisory staff were appointed; there was increased funding for books and equipment and school refurbishing, as well as an extensive INSET programme. The focus of the project was on curriculum, classroom practice and home-school links. Although there were many benefits from the programme as a whole, the independent evaluation carried out by Professor Alexander[12] of Leeds University reported that the failure of the programme to arrest the slight decline in reading standards is attributable in part to the social background of families in inner-city areas and in part to the failure of teachers to move away from a 'deficit model' of children's needs, characterized by low expectations and an unchallenging curriculum. These conclusions are confirmed by a recent study of reading standards in Buckinghamshire which concluded that the sharpest decline in reading standards occurred in the most disadvantaged areas of the county.[13] Alexander's conclusions on this subject are worth quoting in full:

> The impact of poverty on a child's life and prospects is greater than the rather clinical phrase 'social and material disadvantage' can ever convey. The teaching of reading has been in the public arena for some months now and the brunt of the political attack has been borne by primary teachers and teacher trainers. While our evidence underlines the need for a sharpening of the educational response, it also suggests that without a change in the social and economic circumstances which lead to poverty and social dislocation, teachers will continue to fight a losing battle.[14]

A more positive study by Doria Pilling[15] focuses on those young people from the National Child Development Study who did particularly well, despite being socially disadvantaged in childhood. Interviews with these young people at the age of 27 suggested that 'escape from disadvantage' was strongly associated with parental (particularly paternal) support and interest in education and achievement, as well as favourable life experiences and qualities such as persistence, resilience and high achievement motivation.

Despite the research evidence that schools can narrow the achievement gap between pupils from different social backgrounds, many teachers remain pessimistic about the ability of schools to compensate for the effects of poverty and social disadvantage. There is therefore a risk that the abilities of such pupils might be underestimated.

Nor is such pessimism confined to teachers. Even the report of the widely praised Task Group on Assessment and Testing,[16] after briefly summarizing the effect of socio-economic factors on educational attainments concluded that, 'it is difficult to see how such factors can be taken into account in reports of the performance of individual schools'.

Instead, they recommended that the National Curriculum results of individual schools should be 'set in context' by indicating 'the nature of socio-economic and other influences which are known to affect schools and the known influences of such effects on performance'.[17]

This issue has beome timely now that the publication of National Curriculum results has become compulsory and parents are being asked to judge schools by their published results. It is clear that such results will depend a great deal (though not entirely) on the social composition of the catchment areas of the school. Children from prosperous suburbs are likely to achieve better results than those from an inner-city school in an area of poor housing and social deprivation. These differences will affect the initial attainments of children when they first arrive in the school. But the Secretary of State has now ruled that raw results must be published 'without sociological analysis'.

This illustrates the disadvantage of forcing schools to report single, one-shot assessments rather than considering the progress made by a school's pupils over a period of time. On such an analysis, children in the inner-city school might have made relatively much more progress over a three-year period than children in the suburban school. Parents who are now being encouraged to judge schools by their results are therefore going to be given incomplete and misleading information which does justice neither to the strengths nor to the weaknesses of a school.

REDUCING INEQUALITIES

There is a long-standing debate on whether or not education can 'compensate for society'. Inequalities in educational achievements largely, though perhaps not wholly, reflect inequalities in the structure and workings of societies and their institutions. As long as a substantial section of our society lives in poverty and continues to be unemployed, badly housed and fed and disproportionately vulnerable to ill health, there must be limits to what can be achieved by educational intervention alone, however much it is restructured and reformed. But what are these limits and are individual teachers and society as a whole in danger of underestimating what can be achieved?

PRE-SCHOOL PROJECTS

The Headstart movement of the late 1960s in the United States was a massive attempt to combat the educational consequences of disadvantage and poverty by means of a combined strategy of educational intervention for the children and social and economic support for their families and the neighbourhoods in which they were living. When the children in the better run programmes were followed up 20 years later, they were reported to have better educational and social outcomes, compared with children from the same backgrounds who were not exposed to Headstart. Fewer children were referred to special schools or dropped out of school and more remained at school beyond the statutory age. They also had better employment records, lower divorce rates and fewer offences against the law. These remarkable findings can neither be easily explained nor dismissed. We do not know which aspect of the pre-school prgrammes contributed to these better long-term outcomes but the difference between the groups is substantial and no mere statistical artefact.[18]

In this country, the Educational Priority Area project, though inevitably more modest in scope, also produced some positive though less dramatic results.[19] Several other pre-school projects seemed to result in positive gains for children, especially in projects in which there was a clear commitment to working in partnership with parents and in involving them in exploring new ways of playing and talking with their children.

PARTNERSHIP WITH PARENTS

There is clear evidence from these pre-school projects that children benefit most when parents are consulted and actively involved.[20] But can this partnership be extended to the school years?

The case for partnership with parents was powerfully argued by the Plowden Committee in 1967 and also by the Court Committee on Child Health Services which published its report in 1976; 'we have found no better way to raise a child than to reinforce the ability of his parents, whether natural or substitute, to do so'.[21]

These conclusions seem almost trite until one remembers that it was not so long ago that parents were kept at a firm distance from the activities of the classroom. Even today, there are schools with only limited and formal contacts with parents, such as poorly attended parents' evenings or confrontations with parents when there is a problem.

The time is long overdue for all schools and governing bodies to reappraise their policy and practice in the field of home–school links with the aim of forging more effective working relationships with parents and the local community. Such a policy benefits all, particularly the pupils themselves. For example, it is clear that children learn to read faster and with more enjoyment when parents are involved in listening to their children read or when they participate in one of the many 'shared reading' programmes.[22] Furthermore, the evidence suggests that parents from all sections of society respond very positively to approaches from schools, once they are convinced that they will not be criticized or patronized by teachers and that they will be treated as equal partners.[23]

Unfortunately, the goal of home–school partnership has been undermined by the creation of a political climate in which parents have been encouraged to act as watchdogs of teachers and schools, in the name of accountability and parental choice. The siege mentality which this induces in teachers hardly makes for partnership based on equality and shared interests.

Although it is obviously sensible to legislate for greater representation of parents on governing bodies and to require governors to call annual meetings of all parents, the social composition of governing bodies is strongly biased towards middle-class parents. This is partly because of the heavy investment of time required and partly because parents with professional training and with connections with business and industry are much in demand.

There is also some merit in the proposal to make schools more open and to publish information about the curriculum and children's attainments. But publishing league tables assumes that parents will judge schools purely on the basis of test results; the evidence suggests that parents who know and value their local schools will choose on the basis of richer criteria than test results alone. On the other hand, schools that have failed to develop strong working links with parents and with the local community may find themselves disadvantaged when they are forced to publish crude test results or truancy figures.

Many parents of young people in our schools have themselves been failed by the system. It is not surprising that such parents are not enthusiastic about attending parents' meetings or taking part in the life of the school. They often perceive a gap between their own life styles and priorities and those of the teachers with whom they may have little in common. Teachers in their turn receive virtually no preparation on working with parents as equal partners and are also hesitant and lacking in confidence on how to relate to parents in general and to individual parents in particular. The whole area of home–school partnership has not received much priority at any level.

So it is not surprising that there are no national pressure or advocacy groups fighting for the right of underachieving pupils or for the vast majority of pupils with learning or behaviour difficulties. On the other hand, there are powerful lobbies campaigning for various groups of disabled children, such as children who are physically or mentally handicapped who come from all sections of society.

WHO ARE THE CHILDREN WITH SPECIAL EDUCATIONAL NEEDS?

I have concentrated so far on the effects of children's response to schooling of socio-economic factors in general and poverty in particular because there is clear evidence that these factors are strongly linked to underachievement at school. When Sir Keith Joseph was Secretary of State for Education in the early 1980s, he repreatedly drew attention to the 40 per cent of pupils who were failing to benefit from what schools had to offer or, to put it differently, who were being failed by the schools. Nearly all these children come from the poorest and most disadvantaged sections of our society. However, not all of them can be said to be pupils with special educational needs, in the wide sense in which the term is now used.

The Warnock Committee[24] established that one in five children at some time and one in six children at any time should be regarded as having special educational needs. The 1981 Education Act defined such children as having 'significantly greater learning difficulties than the majority of children of their age'. A very small minority of the nation's children are in special schools— around 1.5 per cent at the present time. Most children were already attending ordinary schools in 1978 and there was no intention that they should be anywhere else.

The Warnock Report marked a significant advance in thinking insofar as it saw the causes or origins of special educational needs as not necessarily lying only within the children. Schools, too, could create special educational needs—by virtue of an inaccessible curriculum, by pitching individual lessons at too high a level, by using textbooks or teacher talk that were too difficult to understand. A pupil may have special educational needs in one school but not in another, depending on the accessibility of the curriculum and on the additional support provided for pupils experiencing difficulties.

During the 1980s and long before the National Curriculum was mooted, many schools were seriously re-examining their curriculum from the point of view of access and relevance. Perhaps the best known examples are in the series of reports published by the late Inner London Education Authority, particularly the Hargreaves Report on secondary schools[25] and the Fish Report on special education.[26]

At the same time, funding from the Technical and Vocational Education Initiative helped schools not only to forge links with the community but to reappraise the whole curriculum. More emphasis was placed on personal and social education, on health an careers education, as well as on economic awareness—all later incorporated into the 'whole curriculum' documents in the wake of the 1988 Education Reform Act. In addition, the records of achievement movement developed ways of celebrating all aspects of a pupil's achievements and interests, not just academic and examination attainments. Pupils and parents were involved in the formulation of these records of achievement, which are now to be used for pupils of all ages, including those in special schools.

At national level, the report of the Swann Committee on the education of children from ethnic minorities[27] again focused on the need to start with curriculum reform for all pupils, rather than being pre-occupied with the problems of fitting the existing curriculum to 'minorities', whether these were children with special educational needs or children from ethnic minorities.[28]

Sir Keith Joseph's concern with the 40 per cent of pupils who were leaving school without formal qualifications led to the Lower-Attaining Pupils Programme, aimed specifically at underachieving fourth- and fifth-year secondary pupils. Thirteen LEAs received additional funding to develop projects, activities and experiences which would enhance the motivation and achievements of these pupils and provide a better transition to adult and working life. An initial evaluation by Her Majesty's Inspectorate in 1989[29] reported improvements in the quality of personal and social education and in enhancing the status of work with such pupils in the schools. But the projects seemed to have little effect on attendance rates and many of the schools developed an alternative curriculum which had the effect of segregating these young people from other pupils rather than catering for their needs within a whole-school policy which ensured that the curriculum and activities of the school were accessible to all pupils.[30]

THE EDUCATION REFORM ACT

The question now is whether the Education Reform Act can reduce the gross inequalities of opportunity and achievement which have blighted our education system and the lives of generations of children. Whatever else is claimed for the Education Reform Act, it can hardly be hailed as a charter for minorities, least of all for pupils with special educational needs. Where the 1981 Act was concerned with additional provision and support, the 1988 Act aims to foster excellence and to raise standards all round. Although the Act and the associated circulars and statutory orders make it clear that 'each pupil should have a broad and balanced curriculum that is relevant to his or her particular needs', teachers and parents feel that pupils with special educational needs are very low on the priority list. Special educational needs were originally overlooked altogether; when added as an afterthought, the concern was with exclusion from the National Curriculum rather than with promoting access.

Local Management of Schools (LMS) is still seen as the major threat to meeting special educational needs in ordinary schools. There is a real fear that heads and governors will wish to exclude children who are difficult or expensive to teach and who may 'drag down the school's performance indicators'. There is already evidence of a rise in the number of exclusions and of requests for placement in special schools, particularly of children who are seen as difficult or disruptive.

The work of support teachers is crucial in supporting both pupils with special educational needs and the teachers who work with them. Support teachers also play a key role in helping pupils to transfer from special to ordinary schools and in working with pupils in ordinary schools who might previously have gone to special schools. But LMS casts doubts on how such teachers will be funded: whether LEAs will be able to continue to fund them centrally, and, if not, whether schools will wish to or be able to pay for support services themselves.

The integration of pupils with special educational needs has made patchy progress. The number of pupils in special schools has decreased by less than 10 per cent over the past 10 years. Progress has been much greater for some types of special need than for others and in some parts of the country more than others. For example, the percentage of pupils in special schools varies between 0.6 per cent in places as different as Cornwall and Barnsley to just under 4 per cent in some of the new London boroughs.[31]

Even though we have not made striking progress towards integration, most special schools have forged regular working links with neighbouring ordinary schools, resulting in well planned social and educational contacts between pupils and teachers from both sectors. Here again, LMS raises questions about how such schemes will be funded in the future.

The undermining of the role of LEAs presents particular problems in this field. In the past, LEAs have taken the lead in planning provision for pupils with special educational needs across the whole authority. They have also taken the main initiative in implementing the 1981 Education Act and in making additional provisions for pupils with statements of special educational need. Although they still have a statutory duty to do this, it is difficult to see how they will fulfil their responsibilities with the limited funding and staffing available to them.

Similarly, the decision to abolish Her Majesty's Inspectorate in its present form is a major setback to this field. The special needs inspectorate has issued over 20 national reports during the past two years which have drawn attention to strengths and weaknesses in special needs provision in both ordinary and special schools. They have also issued excellent guidelines on planning and provision not only for schools but also for support services. This cannot be replaced by the kind of local inspection service envisaged by the Government. Furthermore, we do not yet know the criteria by which schools will be inspected under these new arrangements and whether the effectiveness of schools will be judged in part by their success in meeting the needs of the whole range of pupils, including those with learning and behaviour difficulties.

The Government's commitment to grant-maintained schools is another indication of where the priorities lie. For some time it was not even clear whether such schools would be subject to the 1981 Act and, although it was originally laid down that they would not be allowed to change their status, the rules have now been changed to allow them to become selective and to reject unwanted pupils. Pupils with special educational needs are not likely to be welcomed or catered for, nor are LEA support services for such pupils likely to be available in grant-maintained schools not accountable to the LEA.

There are also serious problems over assessment in both ordinary and special schools. The Government has recently changed the rules to make it possible for the ablest pupils to record results above level 3 at the age of seven but seem unwilling to consider a downward extension of National Curriculum assessment for less able pupils who have not yet reached level 1 statements of attainment. As Standard Assessment Tasks (SATs) turn into short paper and pencil tests, they will become less appropriate for more and more pupils.

Despite the many problems raised by the Education Reform Act for pupils with special educational needs, there is clear evidence of a strong determination on the part of teachers in most special and many ordinary schools to ensure that all pupils are given the fullest possible access to the National Curriculum and that exclusion and exemption are kept to the minimum. Dozens of working parties have been set up throughout the country to develop guidelines on how programmes of study and attainment targets can be made accessible to all pupils, including those with profound and multiple disabilities. Some excellent guidelines have been or will soon be published.[32]

Unfortunately, the energy and commitment of teachers has not been matched by the Government, whose priorities seem to be elsewhere. For example, the decision to restrict GCSE coursework against the advice of the profession will undoubtedly reduce the access of less able pupils to GCSE courses. The GCSE was designed to recognize positive achievement for all pupils but the Government has now stopped the examination boards from broadening the grade criteria to the whole 10-level range of the National Curriculum. It looks as though we shall soon return to a divisive system of courses and examinations at 16 which separates the academic from the vocational, at the very time when the undoubted success of the GCSE gave promise of a more integrated and fairer system.

Prospects for young people leaving school are not encouraging. It is well known that one of the failures of our education system is that only around one third of young people continue in full-time education after the age of 16 and that many other European countries have much higher staying-on rates. Although most pupils in special schools tend to remain at school till 18, those with special educational needs in ordinary schools face a very uncertain future. During the 1980s the various Youth Training Schemes did aim to cater for their needs but provision was extremely uneven across the country. Today, the main questions concern the priority which will be given to all young people with special needs in the quasi-independent Colleges of Further Education. HMI has recently criticized the poor transition arrangements between schools and colleges and the lack of support for these students in further education.[33] It remains to be seen what degree of priority and funding will be made available to these young people by the new college governors.

TOWARDS AND BEYOND 2000

Looking to the future, what are the chances that our education system will be more successful in meeting the needs of all children and young people and not just those who are academically successful?

On the positive side of the balance sheet, it is possible that the National Curriculum itself can provide the foundation for a curriculum for all. In order to achieve such a goal, pupils who until now have been failed by the education system will need to be given a much greater degree of priority at every level. Governments will need to translate their own rhetoric into resources and perhaps set up a national advisory body to study the present system and to devise means of improving the quality of provision for such pupils. They will also need to review and possibly revise the 1981 and 1988 Acts to ensure that they are compatible and that monitoring and evaluation mechanisms are established.

With the change in role of HMI and the weakening of LEAs, the future lies with some 30,000 schools and colleges. Schools have already responded very well by undertaking a major review of their curriculum. But they have been hampered by lack of resources, by lack of leadership from their weakened LEAs and by lack of understanding of the needs of pupils with special educational needs at the level of central and sometimes of local government.

All schools need a clear staff development strategy within which all members of the teaching and non-teaching staff have opportunities to develop their knowledge, understanding and skills. But training opportunities are now limited to short, school-based and skill-based courses. Important though these are, there is no time for teachers to reflect, study issues in depth and plan strategically for the future. In our rush to keep pace with the latest innovation, we are failing to train the next generation of leaders.

The establishment of more effective lines of communication between parents and teachers is important for all pupils but particularly for those who are not benefiting as fully as they should. There needs to be much more information-sharing between parents and teachers not only on the curriculum and on how children's assessments compare with other children and other schools but also about their personal and social development, about how to build on children's interests and strengths and how to harness their motivation. We need new forms of dialogue and communication between home and school, and rather less of parents being set up as teacher watchdogs.

The implementation of the 1989 Children Act provides a new opportunity for the development of a more coordinated strategy for meeting the needs of all children by the local authority as a whole and not just the local education authority. For the first time, there is a statutory obligation on Education, Social Services and Health to work together to meet children's needs, to ensure parents' rights and responsibilities and above all to consult young people themselves when special provision is being planned. Children in need are defined as all those children who 'are unlikely to achieve or maintain a reasonable state of health or development without the provision of services by the local authority'. It remains to be seen whether the opportunities to rethink the nature and quality of our provision for children in need will be seized at local level.

In the last analysis, prospects for pupils with special educational needs will reflect the values and priorities of society and of its institutions. These in turn are formed by the quality and accuracy of the information which is available about the progress that has been made and can continue to be made in ensuring that the young people are seen as fellow citizens, with the same rights and the same opportunities as all other children.

Any judgement on the success of our education system should not be confined to concerns with educational standards alone or whether we are better equipped to beat our competitors. Equally important is the contribution of our education service to narrowing the gap between different sectors of society and to providing full and equal access to children and young people from poor and disadvantaged backgrounds. If we can succeed in this task, we will all live in a richer and fairer society.

NOTES

1. DES (1991) *Standards in Education: The Annual Report of HM Senior Chief Inspector of Schools, 1989–90*, p.2, par. 9. London: HMSO.
2. Bradshaw, J. (1990) *Child Poverty and Deprivation in the UK*. London: National Children's Bureau.
3. Townsend, P. (1991) *The Poor are Poorer: A Statistical Report on Changing Living Standards of Rich and Poor in the United Kingdom 1979-1988*. Bristol University: Department of Social Policy and Planning.
4. Townsend, P. and Whitehead, N. (1988) *Inequalities in Health*. London: Penguin.
5. Davie, R., Butler, N. and Goldstein, H. (1972) *From Birth to Seven*. London: Longman.
6. Wedge, P. and Prosser, H. (1973) *Born to Fail?* London: Arrow Books and National Children's Bureau.
7. Essen, J. and Wedge, P. (1982) *Continuities in Childhood Disadvantage*. London: Heinemann.
8. Fogelman, K. (1983) *Growing Up in Great Britain*. London: Macmillan and National Children's Bureau.
9. Rutter, M., Maugham, B., Mortimore, P. and Ouston, D. (1979) *Fifteen Thousand Hours: Secondary Schools and their Effects on Children*. London: Open Books.

10. Mortimore, P., Sammons, P., Ecob, R. and Stoll, L. (1988) *School Matters: The Junior Schools.* Salisbury: Open Books.
11. Smith, D. and Tomlinson, S. (1989) *The School Effect: A Study of Multi-Racial Comprehensives.* London: Policy Studies Institute.
12. Alexander, R. (1991) *Primary Education in Leeds.* Leeds: Leeds University School of Education.
13. Lake, R. (1991) *Reading Standards in Buckinghamshire Primary Schools*, Unpublished report, Bucks County Council.
14. Alexander (1991), p. 53.
15. Pilling, D. (1990) *Escape from Disadvantage.* London: Falmer Press.
16. DES/WO (1987) *Report of the Task Group on Assessment and Testing.* London: HMSO.
17. Ibid, par. 133–5.
18. Haywood, C., Begab, M. and Richardson, S. (eds.) (1981) *Psycho-social Aspects of Retarded Performance.* Baltimore, Md.: University Park Press.
19. Halsey, A. (1972) *Educational Disadvantage.* London: HMSO.
20. Bronfenbrenner, U. (1974) *Is Early Intervention Effective?* Washington, DC: US Department of Health and Welfare.
21. DHSS (1976) *Fit for the Future* (Report of the Court Committee on Child Health Services). London: HMSO.
22. Topping, K. and Wolfendale, S. (1985) *Parental Involvement in Children's Reading.* London: Croom Helm.
23. Widlake, P. (1985) *Reducing Educational Disadvantage.* London: Routledge and Kegan Paul.
24. DES (1978) *Report of the Committee of Enquiry into the Education of Handicapped Children and Young People: Special Educational Needs* (The Warnock Report). London: HMSO.
25. ILEA (1984) *Improving Secondary Education* (The Hargreaves Report). London: ILEA.
26. ILEA (1985) *Equal Opportunities for All?* (The Fish Report). London: ILEA.
27. DES (1985) *Education for All* (The Swann Report). London: HMSO.
28. Mittler, P. (1989) 'Warnock and Swann: Similarities and Differences', in Verma, G. (ed.) *Education for All: A Landmark in Pluralism.* London: Falmer.
29. DES/HMI (1989) *The Lower-Attaining Pupils Programme.* London: HMSO.
30. Stradling, P. and Saunders, H. (1991) *The Lower-Attaining Pupils' Programme: An Evaluation.* Windsor: NFER/Nelson.
31. Swann, W. (1991) *Integration Statistics.* London: Centre for Studies in Integrated Education.
32. See Ashdown, R., Carpenter, B. and Bovair, K. (eds.) (1991) *The Curriculum Challenge: Access to the National Curriculum for Pupils with Severe and Complex Learning Difficulties.* London: Fulton.
33. Fagg, S., Aherne, P., Skelton, S. and Thornber, A. (1990) *Entitlement for All in Practice: A Broad, Balanced and Relevant Curriculum for Pupils with Severe and Complex Learning Difficulties.* London: Fulton.
34. NCC (1991) *Guidance and INSET Materials for Pupils with Severe Learning Difficulties.* York: NCC

Chapter 9

Education for 16- to 19-Year-Olds: Some Proposals for Change

Tessa Blackstone

I was delighted to accept the invitation to contribute to this series of lectures held to mark the anniversary of the launch of the Great Debate on British education in the autumn of 1976. Indeed I was honoured to be asked, as I am sure is true of the other contributors. For me, however, it is a special pleasure, since 15 years ago I was a member of the Central Policy Review Staff in the Cabinet Office working behind the scenes as a policy adviser. In this privileged position I observed the launch of the Great Debate from inside government and even, in a very small way, contributed from the back room. In particular I remember enjoying the role of goad and tease of the Department of Education and Science (DES), whose senior officials and Her Majesty's Inspectors (HMI) were not altogether happy with Jim Callaghan's splendid initiative. My job in the Think Tank was to work on the follow-up to the Prime Minister's Ruskin Speech and to comment on the rather turgid draft papers to emerge from the DES, which were designed to take the debate further. I would like to thank Lord Callaghan for providing me this opportunity. It was challenging as well as fun and allowed me to escape back into social and educational policy from the Review of Overseas Representation, which was my main preoccupation at the time.

THE CONTINUING AGENDA: 16- TO 19-YEAR-OLDS

In his opening speech of this series, Lord Callaghan said that the debate on aims, methods, structure and content had hardly stopped since then. How right he is. However, the stage of education on which least progress has been made, and about which there is now a new Great Debate taking place, is provision for 16- to 19-year-olds. For many years it was neglected by educationalists and policy-makers alike. Today it is very much on the agenda, as it should be, although it is beset by unresolved problems, which the Government has failed to address adequately. In 1988 the Education Reform Act, by far the largest piece of legislation affecting education since the 1944 Act, left this stage of education virtually untouched; this was an extraordinary omission on the part of the Government. Nor is the omission adequately rectified by the Bill on Further and Higher Education currently going through Parliament.

The failure to educate young people in this age group is now giving rise to mounting criticism with dissatisfaction being expressed in many quarters. It was given particular prominence by Sir Claus Moser in his Presidential Address to the British Association in August 1990[1] in which he called for a Royal Commission on Education. It has been the subject of severe criticism by the CBI and by the TUC. Individual representatives of the commercial and industrial world, such as David Sainsbury[2] in his 1990 TSB Lecture, have referred to it as a national disgrace. In the last year or so, many other organizations have entered the fray and are calling for reform. They include the Royal Society, the Royal Society of Arts, the Secondary Heads Association, the Association of Principals of Sixth Form Colleges, the Committee of Vice-Chancellors and Principals, the Institute of Physics, the Advisory Council on Science and Mathematics, the Institute of Directors, the CBI, the TUC and many others.

At the heart of the problem is the fact that far too many young people leave full-time education at 16. The statistics are immensely depressing. Only 54 per cent of 16-year-olds and 37 per cent of 17-year-olds stay on in full-time education. Only 16 per cent of young people obtain 2 or more passes at GCE A-Level—the main route into higher education. These statistics hide huge regional and social class differences; in Harrow 77 per cent stay in full-time education after the age of 16; in Tyneside only 35 per cent do so. Only 5 per cent of 18-year-olds from manual backgrounds go into higher education. The Government claims staying-on rates are improving. They are. But they have been improving even faster in other countries. Only Greece has worse staying-on rates amongst EC countries. In Scandinavia, in France, in the USA and in Japan the proportion staying on is hugely greater than in Britain, with Japan at the top of the league with nearly 90 per cent of 18-year-olds in full-time education. Why are we doing so badly?

The nature of the labour market and the structure of the education system both contribute to our undeniable failure. Many employers consciously or unconsciously encourage young people to leave. They pay relatively high wages. They run training schemes which require young recruits to enter them by a certain age, making potential older entrants ineligible. The acquisition of skills, especially broader-based skills and further educational qualifications, is not rewarded adequately to provide young people with a direct incentive to acquire them. Employers compete for well-qualified 16- and 17-year-old school leavers, turning them away from further study. The labour market for this age group in European countries such as France and Germany is quite different; there are fewer incentives to enter it.

DIVISION AND DIVISIVENESS

Turning to the education system and its contribution to the problem, we are faced with a divided system and, as a consequence, a divisive system. The academic route is far too specialized and too narrow in relation to the skills it tests. Vocational education and training is incoherent and confusing with too many competing qualifications. It is also too narrow and too job-specific in many respects. The existence of the two separate systems leads to a process of weeding out the majority of pupils who are deemed unsuitable for the academic route and therefore for higher education. This weeding out is on a massive scale: 75 per cent of pupils are excluded from the A-Level starting line; 85 per cent of pupils fail to get to the A-Level finishing line defined as two passes. The qualification system is an obstacle course in which academic pupils are separated from the rest, pursuing different qualifications in different institutions with different curricula. And it is difficult for those who have been weeded out to get back in again.

Most commentators seeking solutions to the problem of Britain's early selection/low participation system have concentrated on separate sets of reforms for academic and for vocational education. For example, the Higginson Report[3] advocated a broadening of A-Levels; and a new streamlined system of National Vocational Qualifications (NVQs) is being introduced. These reforms or proposals for reform are undoubtedly an improvement on the system up to now. But are they the right solution? An alternative approach is to replace the divided system by a new unified system rather than reforming it by various modifications. The problems of early selection and low participation are so deep rooted that, short of far-reaching and radical reforms, they will continue. Tinkering with the existing system will not be enough. To achieve a much better educated population, what is required is a late selection/high participation system. The Institute for Public Policy Research (IPPR) report on a British Baccalaureat[4] advocates a unified system. Its recommendations are designed to encourage greater staying on in full-time education and to ensure that those who leave at 16 will be able to continue to receive education part-time.

A BRITISH BACCALAUREAT

What is being proposed is a new unified system, having the high participation characteristics just identified, and establishing a new approach to vocational competence and to academic standards, which integrates them effectively. The new system would have three linked stages comprising Foundation, Advanced and Higher Stages. There would be explicit overlap between them with opportunities for credit accumulation. The Foundation Stage would mainly cater for 14- to 17-year-olds and would be more or less equivalent to GCSE but would cover low achievers over 16. It would replace BTEC First award, CPVE and various RSA and CGLI awards. The Advanced Stage would lead to the Advanced Diploma which would replace A-Levels and vocational qualifications below HNC. The Higher Stage would cover first degrees and higher vocational awards, which are not the subject of the report. The centrepiece of the proposed reforms is a new Advanced Diploma or British Baccalaureat which would replace A-Levels and the plethora of vocational qualifications, including BTEC Diplomas and Certificates, and would usually be taken at age 18.

The nature of the system of qualifications is the key to the level of participation. Qualifications select, set standards of knowledge and competence and empower. Qualifications that focus on early rather than late selection will reduce participation. Low levels of participation also result from the form of standard-setting for 16- to 19-year-olds that currently prevails. It is implicit and exclusive. It involves a minimal feedback with a single grade often summing up an individual's performance. It depends on failure rates as a guarantee of standards. These characteristics make it difficult to identify improvements in overall standards or to help low achievers do better. Qualifications should instead be explicit in their criteria of achievement, report extensively on individual performance and be based on standards independent of failure rates. Young people are more likely to stay in education if they are offered a more active role in the learning process, some choice and are able to discuss with their teachers the shape of their individual programmes. In other words qualifications should play an empowering role in order to encourage high participation.

The new system proposed by the IPPR is designed to maximize flexibility. Students will be able to learn at different speeds. They will be allowed to go on to more advanced stages in subjects or areas where they are strong. Thus there will be a flexible rather than rigid interface between the Foundation and Advanced Stages. There will be multiple entry and exit in which students' performance can be recognized for internal progress into the Advanced Diploma as well as for external use in the labour market.

The Advanced Diploma would be based on a modular system with an educational core and subject-based options and could be available to those already at work as well as those in full-time education. The IPPR Report lists its aims as follows:

1. Maximize flexibility and choice to appeal to as many students as possible: we are particularly concerned to attract students in the second and third quartile of achievement at 16 who are currently dissuaded from staying on by the rigidities of A-Levels and narrow vocational courses.

2. Allow breadth of study within a core to enable students to pursue a wide range of careers and further specialist study: students who have completed the Diploma should have a wider range of options open to them at 18 than do today's students with A-Levels or specialist vocational awards.

3. Provide the foundations of knowledge necessary for all citizens in a modern democratic society, including an understanding of changes in the organization of work and the design and uses of technology.

4. Offer opportunities for students to specialize and to see how their studies are related to other activities and areas: the Advanced Diploma will combine some specialization, in the sciences, arts or an applied field, with contextual studies that complement their particular specialization.

5. Encourage students to relate theory and practice to bring out the relationship between the two: work or community-based experience will provide an opportunity for all students to use their theoretical studies in a practical context.

The curriculum could be organized in three main areas or 'domains': Social and Human Sciences including history, social science and applied areas such as business studies or health; Natural Sciences and Technology, including maths, science and engineering and skill-based modules; Arts, Languages and Literature including the performing and visual arts and design, as well as languages, literature and media studies.

In each of these domains there would be three types of module and, to obtain the diploma, students would have to complete a minimum number in each category. *Core modules,* which may be theoretical or applied in emphasis, would cover the compulsory content of the Diploma. There would, however, be enough of these core modules to allow choice within each domain. *Specialist modules* again might be theoretical or more applied, e.g. pure maths or database management, allowing choice about the focus of in-depth study. The third *Work/Community-based modules* would be taken by all students. Those leaving school at 16 and going into a work-based trainee scheme would be able to use their employment experience to count for assessment in work-based modules.

All students would need counselling along with career advice on the package of modules they choose. They would be encouraged to combine applied, practical and theoretical elements, choosing at least two modules from each domain. There would be a requirement to take theoretical and applied core modules in each domain. At least one work/community-based module would also be a requirement. The level of difficulty attempted by each student would depend on the student's previous level of attainment and other modules taken.

ASSESSMENT AND CERTIFICATION

This leads to the vital issue of assessment. Above all, a reformed system should judge performance according to agreed standards with clear and public benchmarks of achievement. In other words it should be criterion-referenced. This would involve a move towards more internal in-course assessment, which would help to motivate students and to provide them with feedback, though some external assessment should be maintained to help ensure even standards across the country. Any scheme will need to recognize different levels of attainment as a guide to student progress and the attainment of required standards. The reporting of results will be needed in line with a more student-centred approach. Finally, part-time students would be able to have their employment experience assessed as part of the Diploma.

The aim of this new unified system, with the Advanced Diploma at its centre, will be to help *all* young people develop their critical faculties, become creative, be able to respond to change and indeed initiate change. Job-specific training to meet immediate needs should be provided for adults once a sound educational base has been established. But education for all young people should have some applied elements. These reforms would be of benefit to the economy by encouraging far more young people to stay in education and by developing their potential to acquire more complex skills. They would also provide educational opportunities for the whole population, replacing the divisive and socially unjust system that exists today. They cannot be introduced overnight. They require considerable preparation in a period of transition, as well as the allocation of extra resources. It would, however, be time and money well spent. We can ill afford to muddle on with our present system, dropping further and further behind other countries with respect to staying-on rates.

This has been recognized by the Labour Party, which is committed to introducing a unified system leading to an Advanced Certificate of Education if it wins the General Election. It will incorporate all the existing NVQs at level 5 as well as the Higginson proposal for a 5-subject A-Level. The present Government regrettably rejects this approach. It now advocates the introduction of an Advanced Diploma but this is apparently to be little more than an umbrella for the continuing mish-mash of vocational qualifications on the one hand and A-Levels and AS-Levels on the other. All it appears to be engaged in is a relabelling of existing examinations. It is neither focusing properly on the over-specialization of the present A-Levels nor dealing with the uncoordinated jungle of vocational qualifications. Ministers keep referring to A-Levels as the 'gold standard', at the same time arguing that there can be parity of esteem between academic and vocational qualifications—itself a contradiction in terms. Led initially by their previous prime minister, Mrs Thatcher, they have continued to hang on to the idea that any change to A-Levels will lead to a lowering of standards. They should listen to the experts. By this I mean not HMI or trendy educationalists, who they are so fond of deriding, but their own Advisory Council on Science and Technology, who in a recent report[5] pointed out that

> Advanced (A) level courses in S & T subjects are unattractive to many young people. They place too much emphasis on learning facts at the expense of understanding fundamental scientific principles and the development of scientific skills. The restricted number of A-Levels which it is feasible for most students to take also reduces the scope for arts students to be scientifically educated and for science students to develop wider communications and other personal skills.

The Government apparently wants to go on with a divided system emphasizing two routes into higher education at 18+. At the same time it is clearly unhappy with some aspects of the existing qualifications on the vocational side. Its latest initiative is to introduce yet another one. These are General National Vocational Qualifications (GNVQs). Their purpose is to provide more basic education than the existing NVQs, about which there is growing dissatisfaction because they are too job-specific and narrow. At their core are rather narrowly defined competences—to use the jargon. The problem is that what we need are capable people—not just people with competences. Adding GNVQs into the already overloaded qualification system seems likely to confuse rather than to clarify and yet again fails to grasp the nettle of reforming the divided system. Parents and students alike will be left uncertain about which of the many routes to take and about where they will lead.

INSTITUTIONS AND CONTROL

Let me turn now from the subject of the content of 16 to 19 education and how young people should be assessed to the question of structures. The Government has just introduced a Bill into Parliament which establishes new frameworks for further education and higher education. Indeed the Bill is all about structures with little reference to content—a sad lost opportunity. I would like to take a little time on that part of the Bill concerned with further education, which is of vital importance to the education and training of 16- to 19-year-olds.

The most significant structural change the Bill proposes is the removal of further education from local government control. When the White Paper *Education and Training for the 21st Century*[6] which preceded the Bill was published in the summer, it was apparent to any intelligent commentator that the decision to remove further education from local government was little more than a cynical way of taking over £2 billion out of local government expenditure to help the Government out of its difficulties with the poll tax. And I repeat today that this was unquestionably one of the Government's main motives in introducing this change.

Desperately trying to justify it at the time and since the summer, the Government has used the analogy of the polytechnics being taken out of LEA control by the 1988 Act. It is a false analogy. The polytechnics are large national institutions; some are now considerably larger than many universities. They draw a substantial proportion of their students from all over the country and increasing numbers from abroad. By contrast the further education colleges are local institutions. Their 16 to 19 students mainly live at home; their part-time adult students are in local employment or married women returning to study who are again locally based. Thus they serve a local population and local employers with respect to their training needs. When the polytechnics were removed from local authority control they had had a substantial period of time when the National Advisory Body on Higher Education helped to prepare them for their new status, and established a common funding basis. This provided the new Polytechnics and Colleges Funding Council with useful experience to guide it. The further education sector will not have the advantage of this experience; the new Funding Councils will instead have to start from scratch devising new funding mechanisms—not just for 34 polytechnics but for well over 500 local institutions. The comparison with the polytechnics is spurious and it is time the Government stopped using it. It would also be more honest if ministers stopped suggesting that as a result of their removal from LEA control the polytechnics have suddenly been set free to expand, thereby meeting the national need for more higher education places. The truth of the matter is that the polytechnics expanded greatly and developed many exciting new courses under LEA control. But the Government will not admit this because it is pursuing a vendetta against local government and wants to go on eroding its powers and reducing its functions. Its embarrassing problems caused by the poll tax and its dislike of local government are the reasons it is taking further education away from the local authorities. It is not doing so on good educational grounds.

Conservative councillors all over the country are increasingly disillusioned by what is happening, and they have made it clear in responding to the latest attack on their role. Replies to the consultation document from Tory local authorities were not just critical; they were also angry. Perhaps that is why the Secretary of State has refused to make available the responses to the White Paper. Reasons of national security cannot explain why the normal practice of placing replies to Consultative Documents in the House of Commons Library has been ignored. Abandoning the normal practice suggests that the Government does not want us to know what the consensus of opinion on these proposals is.

No one would dispute the need for further education colleges to get on with their job without petty interference or unnecessary restrictions on their day-to-day management. However, under the Government's own proposals for Local Financial Management, introduced in the Education Reform Act, colleges' governing bodies now already have considerable autonomy. To reorganize the whole system in order to allow colleges to manage their own affairs is a classic case of sledgehammers being used to crack nuts. It will result in serious disruption in the short term and the loss of the capacity to plan this stage of education. Moreover, the centralization proposed is a complete repudiation of the concept of local democratic accountability for what is and should be local a service meeting local needs. The Secretaries of State for Education and for Wales will increase their powers yet again under the Bill. There are countless examples, running all the way through the Bill from beginning to end. They are also to choose the members of the Funding Councils and the regional committees, extending patronage at the expense of electing people on a democratic basis. There is currently no provision for either LEA representation or TEC representation on the Funding Councils.

Extensive local knowledge, experience, and expertise will be squandered in favour of an unaccountable central bureaucracy with an ill-defined regional structure involving the invention of further bureaucracy. A lot of time and expense will have to be devoted to establishing, staffing, and financing these quangos at national and regional levels to carry out tasks at present undertaken perfectly adequately in local government. This is inefficient and uneconomical. The transitional costs are £28 million and the running costs £32 million quite apart from unspecified extra costs in the colleges. The proposals also threaten to destroy local coherence, with responsibility for education and training for those over 16 being divided between a number of bodies. Coherent local planning for 16 to 19s has already been made more difficult by the introduction of grant-maintained schools and city technology colleges outside the LEA control. It will now become even more difficult as a result of the new structure for further education colleges. Strategic leadership will be divided between two Secretaries of State, the Funding Councils and their regional committees, 70 TECs, the governors of 500 colleges and a multitude of examining and awarding boards.

Let me turn first to the divorce that is being introduced between the sixth forms in schools on the one hand and the sixth form colleges and further education colleges on the other. The inclusion of the sixth form colleges in the new sector is particularly perverse. They are small institutions, which are legally schools rather than further education colleges and seen as such by parents and children. It seems unlikely that they will survive in the new sector. But perhaps that is the Government's intention? But not only is their future threatened, so also is the future of sixth forms in schools. Transferring the duty to provide sufficient full-time education for all 16- to 18-year-olds to the new Councils is causing considerable concern in LEAs and 11 to 18 schools about the future of sixth forms. Will they receive the funding necessary to maintain them or is it the Government's intention that they should eventually wither away? If they are to continue, it is not clear how duplication between sixth forms under the LEAs on the one hand and further education or sixth form colleges under the new Councils on the other will be avoided. Nor is it clear how the Government intends to ensure the necessary links are forged both to avoid duplication and to facilitate the sensible transfer of students from one to the other.

The second split concerns the Training and Enterprise Councils. There has been increasing cooperation between the TECs and the LEAs with sensible links being forged. It is a great pity that this growing cooperation will now become more or less irrelevant. The TECs are bound to feel frustrated at having to start again with a new network of regional councils, or with a somewhat remote national council.

Finally, on the subject of links, local authority representatives are to be left off college governing bodies as well as the Funding Councils. No reason is given for this change in the law. It looks like petty discrimination. Even though it will be possible to co-opt them, surely it would be desirable to have them there by right as representatives of the local community and to provide a link into the LEA school system? Why be so dismissive about people with a useful background and a wish to contribute? Students are also to be left off further education governing bodies. The Government claims to be interested in the rights of the consumer and keeps producing Citizen's Charters of one kind or another. Is it not inconsistent with its philosophy to change the law on student representation?

FREE PROVISION?

One of the principles to which LEAs have attached importance is that further education colleges should provide free full-time education for their students in the same age range as those still at school, although that judgement does not derive from primary legislation. Unfortunately institutions in the new further education sector created by the Bill, including sixth form colleges, will not be covered by the legislation which secures the right to free education at school. The Further Education Funding Councils do not have particular powers to determine the charging policy of institutions in the new sector. There must be a risk, therefore, that, over time, institutions will be tempted to levy charges so that within the new sector the principles of free full-time education up to the age of 19 will be eroded. Competition for students will not necessarily safeguard against this risk since in some areas there will not be competing school-based sixth forms offering free education to the 16- to 18-year-olds. There is thus new concern that the educational entitlement of young people may be reduced as an accidental by-product of administrative change, and may indeed vary from locality to locality depending on the decisions made by each institution.

New provisions in the Bill allow schools to charge for part-time students over the age of 16 and full-time students over the age of 19. I am sorry that the principle of free education in secondary schools is being abandoned and I believe many people will be worried by what looks like creeping privatization.

The Bill also fails to provide for an adequate system of monitoring standards in our further education colleges. It merely proposes that the new Councils must appoint quality assessment committees to make arrangements for the quality of the courses for which they are responsible. The provisions are vague and it is unclear how they will work. Nor are we told what, if any, link they will have with HMI or the new inspector arrangements for schools in the Schools Bill which has recently been introduced in the House of Commons. One great advantage of further education colleges being under LEA control is that they are on the spot to intervene when there are problems with respect of quality and standards. It is noteworthy that HMI have been satisfied with the way LEAs have carried out their duties in this respect.

There is just one other aspect of the Bill on which I want to comment. Providing education for 16- to 19-year-olds should be based on concern for young people of all abilities, including those with learning difficulties and those with special needs as a result of physical handicaps. Unfortunately the interests of young people in this category are threatened by the Bill. The Bill requires the new Funding Councils 'to have regard' to the needs of young people with learning difficulties. This is a weaker formulation than the existing duties of LEAs under the 1981 Education Act for pupils in schools and sixth form colleges. It is a missed opportunity to extend the provisions of the 1981 Act to further education colleges and to part-time students who are not covered. There is no provision for any independent review of the requirements of individuals or for the right of appeal against either the level or quality of support for students with special educational needs. It is hardly surprising that every pressure group representing those with disabilities is up in arms. The educational needs of an especially vulnerable group of young people are not being properly addressed.

A TERTIARY SOLUTION

In making all these criticisms of the Government's latest attempts at education reform I do not wish to give the impression that the existing structures are by any means perfect. For example, all over the country there are 11 to 18 schools with small sixth forms, which cannot provide the range of facilities or the range of courses needed to make staying on attractive to the young person of the 1990s. There is a good case for focusing our efforts on providing education for those beyond the school leaving age in separate institutions from schools, whether we call them sixth form colleges, tertiary colleges or further education colleges. I have long believed that institutions providing for 11- and 12-year-olds have difficulty in providing at the same time an appropriate environment for 17- and 18-year-olds. Many young people find seven years in one institution too long in any case. They want to enter a more adult world than they perceive a secondary school to be. They need specialist facilities in the form of high-quality counselling on careers, and on the range of courses available in higher education. This is particularly true of girls, who tend to undervalue their own potential, choosing from too narrow a range of courses or careers, and plumping for something at a lower level than they are capable of achieving. The creation of the Advanced Diploma, allowing young people to choose from a range of modular courses with the possibility of different mixes of theoretical or academic and practical or vocational, will mean institutions with larger numbers of young people than in typical sixth forms. To produce the range of opportunities being proposed and to provide the staff, the accommodation and the equipment needed on an efficient and cost-effective basis requires a large student population. In the light of all these factors, some kind of 'tertiary' solution seems the right one.

Whilst I have argued that LEAs are the right bodies to plan 16 to 19 education in their areas, I will not pretend that some LEAs have not been unnecessarily interfering in the day-to-day running of further education colleges. To guard against that in the future, the Labour Party intends to make it possible for LEAs to have corporate status. It would do this only after consultation with colleges' governing bodies and with the LEAs on how to implement the system. It is the Party's view that this is the best way to guarantee the colleges' autonomy and to maintain the local authorities' role in strategic planning for the education of this age group.

CONCLUSION

In his lecture at the start of this series Lord Callaghan said:

> Too many 16-year-olds leave school alienated from its influence and with little or no desire to continue learning. Unless we devise a firm structure of continued education and training to enable them to make a successful transition from school to work, the potential capability of many 16- to 19-year-olds will never be fulfilled.

I endorse every word of this. I also agree with Lord Callaghan when he says that it will not be possible to motivate a young person from a disadvantaged background 'to continue seriously with education and training if he has little or no expectation of a job at the end of it'. At the beginning of this lecture I complained about the attitudes and practices of some employers with respect to the education and training of young people. But inadequate employment is better than no employment. Continuing high levels of youth unemployment in some parts of the country will bedevil our attempts to increase successful participation in post-school education.

Whether unemployment is high or low, the participation in full-time education of young people over the age of 16 ought to be on a voluntary basis. I would not favour raising the school leaving age. Conscripting into further education would not be a good basis for creating a climate in which young people can learn or be motivated to learn. It would, however, be unrealistic to assume that every young man or woman will stay on even when the changes I have been advocating to make staying on more attractive have been introduced. There will always be some youngsters at this stage of life in revolt against parents and teachers or unable to commit themselves to the discipline of learning. For them we must devise new strategies to bring them back into education as adults when they have matured and when they themselves can see the benefits it may bring them. But that is a subject for another lecture. What I am convinced of, is that for every young person who cannot settle into full-time education at the age of 16 or 17 there are many, many more who can, if only we offer them the right environment to do so. Our failure to restructure employment, and above all our failure to create the right kind of educational institutions and to reform the system of qualifications and the content of education for this age group is still letting too many of them down. And in letting them down we are failing the community as a whole.

NOTES

1.   Moser, C. (1990) *Our Need for an Informed Society*, Presidential Address. London: British Association.
2.   Sainsbury, D. (1990) *Education for Wealth Creation*. London: TSB Group plc.

3.   Higginson Committee (1988) *Advancing A Levels*. London: HMSO.
4.   Finegold, D., Keep, E., Miliband, D., Raffe, D., Spours, K. and Young, M. (1990)*A British Baccalaureat*. London: Institute for Public Policy Research.
5.   ACOST (1991) *Science and Technology: Education and Employment*. London: Advisory Council on Science and Technology.
6.   DES (1991) *Education and Training for the 21st Century*. London: HMSO.

Chapter 10

Education in Wales: A Different 'Great Debate'?

Gareth Elwyn Jones

In the reign of the first Elizabeth there was a great debate about education. Tutor to the young Queen was Roger Ascham, author of *The Scholemaster*.[1] This book resulted from a long discussion over dinner at Windsor in 1563. Dinner was taken in Sir William Cecil's room and the group included Sir Walter Mildmay, Chancellor of the Exchequer, Sir Richard Sackville, Treasurer of the Exchequer, Mr Haddon, the Master of the Court of Requests, a bishop, Ascham and a few others. Ascham recalled it like this—and it might be salutary to inform some of our present Secretaries of State:

> Mr. Secretary hath this accustomed manner, though his head be never so full of most weighty affairs of the realm, yet at dinner time he doth seem to lay them always aside: and findeth ever fit occasion to talk pleasantly of other matters, but most gladly of some matter of learning: wherein he will courteously hear the mind of the meanest at his table.[2]

The conversation ranged widely. Cecil himself was a Tory 'wet':

> Diverse scholars of Eton be run away from the school for fear of beating...whereupon Mr. Secretary took occasion to wish that some more discretion were in many schoolmasters in using correction than commonly there is...whereby many scholars that might else prove well, be driven to hate learning before they know what learning meaneth: and so are made willing to forsake their books and be glad to be put to any other kind of living.[3]

Inevitably the Rhodes Boyson wing was represented too: 'Mr. Haddon was full of Mr. Peters' opinion, and said that the best schoolmaster of our time was the greatest beater.'[4] It may or may not be significant that Ascham records that Sir Walter Mildmay, the Chancellor of the Exchequer, said very little and Sir Richard Sackville, the Treasurer of the Exchequer, said nothing at all. Perhaps, after all, if great debate is not new, the parameters have changed.

Ascham's conversation at dinner focused quite naturally on Eton. There was no Welsh Eton, nor any education in the 'dominion and principality of Wales' which would have exercised the great minds of state. Today there are commentators whose frame of reference has changed little. Sample the substantial education section in Dillons bookshop in Malet Street, serving London's university. See if you get any impression that the Education Reform Act of 1988 applies to two countries, not one. See if you can find a reference to Wales in the index of the 1100 pages of the *Encyclopedia of Contemporary Education*. This series of lectures included an inspirational lecture given by Professor Richard Pring (Chapter 6). He provided us with an alphabet soup of educational bodies and qualifications which was both amusing and frightening. It did not include the initials CCW (Curriculum Council for Wales). To take a more surprising example, in a collection of essays edited by Moon[5] on the National Curriculum we have, quite rightly, a black perspective on it from Conrad MacNeil.[6] He starts his essay thus.

> The proposed National Curriculum is not truly national. The culture reflected in it is no more than prevailing white Anglo-Saxon and totally excludes the significant input from the Caribbean, the African and Indian continents and elsewhere.[7]

There is nothing in the whole book—nor in many like it—to indicate that 'England and Wales' is anything other than a homogeneous mass. Such an attitude is not acceptable.

I want to argue first that, in looking at the wider context of the debate surrounding the Ruskin College speech and its aftermath, we work our way towards a significant Welsh dimension, one which is usually totally unappreciated. Secondly, that focusing exclusively on the one obviously Welsh debate, that over the Welsh language, is wholly inadequate. And finally, that some of the changes which have come about as a result of the Great Debate have given us in Wales unprecedented opportunities to enhance the Welsh dimension of education in its widest sense.

THE RUSKIN COLLEGE SPEECH: ISSUES IDENTIFIED

First, let me briefly recapitulate the issues which Lord Callaghan highlighted in his speech[7] in October 1976. First, there was concern over 'methods and aims of informal instruction ...'. Secondly, there was a 'strong case for the so-called core curriculum of basic knowledge'. Thirdly, there was the question of 'monitoring the use of resources in order to maintain a proper national standard of performance'. Fourthly, linked with standards, there was 'the role of the inspectorate in relation to national standards and their maintenance'. Fifthly, there was 'the need to improve relations between industry and education'. Finally, there was the problem of the examination system.

It is necessary only to recite the litany of issues to see why it turned out to warrant the epithet of the 'Great Debate'. All have been confronted head-on or tangentially since. It would, of course, be wholly unrealistic to argue that the contexts of the debate in England and in Wales were completely dissimilar. The broad economic and political contexts in the two countries have much in common, inevitably when they share the same central government. But I want to argue that there is many a Welsh dimension to be uncovered if we probe a little below the surface.

THE EDUCATIONAL CONTEXT

I turn to just a few of the contexts in which the Ruskin speech was made, beginning with some brief, banal points about the educational context.

First, there had been a wholesale change to a system of comprehensive secondary schools in much of England and virtually all of Wales and the consequent liberation of primary schools from the 11-plus straitjacket. It carried with it the logic of mixed-ability teaching in primary and secondary schools, and a common examination system at 16-plus. This change was, therefore, the catalyst, one of the most significant changes in the post-industrial history of education.

Secondly, there continued to be ideological and practical debate over the curriculum, particularly the primary school curriculum, in the 1960s and the 1970s, ranging widely from the child-centred romantics to the 'cultural transmission' conservatives, with some who saw the curriculum as an instrument to enhance the cause of social justice thrown in for good measure.

Thirdly, there had been, arguably, a change of orthodoxy as a result of the Plowden Report in 1967,[8] with child-centred methods becoming the 'accepted' approach.

Fourthly, the result was that there was experimentation, and there was, just as important, a rhetoric of experimentation. This resulted in a backlash in the 1960s and 1970s. Some of it consisted of genuine concerns about lack of structure in the curriculum. Some of it, even in the Black Papers,[9] was profound and interesting. Some of it was tabloid-type nonsense.

Finally, the response to experimentation and its critics took a variety of forms. There was an attempt to evaluate teaching styles more objectively and in a more conceptually sophisticated way. Neville Bennett's work,[10] for example, was followed by Her Majesty's Inspectorate (HMI)[11] reporting on teaching styles. Another response was the promulgation of the idea of a core curriculum. A third response was to give in to demands for evaluation, with the establishment of the Assessment of Performance Unit (APU) in 1974.

Where was Wales in all this? Very early on, many moons before Plowden[12]—and we tend to forget that there was child-centred life before 1967—Wales was seemingly set on exactly the same course as England. It is fascinating to contrast the post-war curricular adventurousness, with its emphasis on individual growth born out of the anti-fascism of the war, with later anguished cries of 'back to basics'. In 1949 the Central Advisory Council for Wales[13] reported that:

> Growth implies activity. Activity then should be the pervading quality of school life. The curricula of secondary schools should be based upon activities. Hitherto the tradition of the secondary schools in Wales, and in other countries, has been one of constrained assimilation of knowledge.

The report went on to wax lyrical about there being 'the least impediment to initiative' and that it was in the 'spirit of creative Christian humanism that we wish to approach the curricula of grammar-technical and modern-technical schools in this new era in Wales'. It did not happen in the secondary schools.

How far did such an approach permeate the primary schools of Wales? The basics of reading and writing, the alleged shortcomings of which have produced so much acrimony in England, do not seem to have produced such difficulties in Wales, not even in the last few years. A recent HMI survey[14] reports: 'In a substantial majority of schools (over four-fifths) standards of reading are satisfactory.' 'The early stages of writing are effectively taught and most pupils achieve satisfactory standards.' It is fascinating that it is the imaginative writing and poetry which were inadequate, hardly the stuff of Black Paper and Centre for Policy Studies nightmares. Lest this latest judgement be seen as some kind of reaction to recent pressures we can turn to another HMI (Wales) survey,[15] of 1984. The criticism was that too much attention was being paid to the basic skills: 'In many classes there is a strongly held view that pupils must master certain 'basic' skills before they can move on to work which requires independent learning and the use of those basic skills.' HMI summary is unequivocal.

> In most primary schools considerable prominence is given to certain aspects of language and mathematics and much less prominence to most other areas of the curriculum...within individual classes the general pattern of organisation is for the mornings to be devoted to work in language and mathematics and for the afternoons to be devoted to the remaining curriculum areas.[16]

Presumably trendy Plowden, even Gittins,[17] fads were being implemented only east of Offa's Dyke.

THE POLITICAL CONTEXT

It is a truism that educational debate in the 1970s took on an increasingly political dimension and the Ruskin College speech symbolizes this. But I do not accept the historical framework almost invariably erected to accommodate that truism. I have never been convinced by the consensus model of post-1944 educational change, and, equally, I do not really understand the usually accepted notion of the breakdown of consensus since the 1970s.

The Black Paper of 1975[18] and the Ruskin College speech raised the same issues—teaching according to set syllabuses and specific standards of attainment and an emphasis on literacy and numeracy. Certainly, partial privatization of the schools in the wake of 1988 has been the result of party political dogma; but insofar as the Great Debate was about, and ended up with, curricular standardization, it represented a kind of consensus among the political parties.

In response to the Ruskin College speech which, for the moment, had upstaged the Conservatives' increased concern to point out that they were the party of standards and excellence in education, they mounted a variety of campaigns to wrest back the initiative. So we have the two parties with not dissimilar concerns, and a general acceptance that the Ruskin College speech was the occasion on which 'the grandiose claims of the sixties were replaced...by more sober, pragmatic purposes'.[19] Education was not going to transform the economy or produce social equality. Neither was it, for many commentators, any longer doing its traditional job of passing on the cultural heritage. So, by 1976 the many-pronged attack on the shortcomings, for some the positive harm, of the developments of the 1960s was sufficiently well-rooted to produce a kind of political convergence.

The Ruskin College speech showed Labour's concern. There were other strategies from the Opposition, pursued relentlessly by Conservative pressure groups through the 1980s. There were accusations of widespread illiteracy and innumeracy in young employees, for example. The alleged lack of general knowledge provided a bit of light relief. In a December 1987 issue of *The Observer*[20] we were informed that,

> A board (the Associated Examining Board) survey reveals that candidates in previous geography tests put Snowdonia in Scotland, Everest in Africa and Canada in Europe. Asked to name the river that starts near the Equator in melting snow, supplies the Aswan Dam and flows northwards through a desert for more than 1,000 miles, one candidate wrote; 'River Dee'...Mr. Kevin McGrath, director of vocational education at the Association of British Travel Agents national Training Board (no less) said...his criticism was not of geography teachers but of the system [sic]. Geography in school tended to be concept-based, not knowledge-based. Children could tell you what type of soil the Mid-West of America had without knowing where it was.

So the case for devising a national system of testing which would ensure that all children realised that the Mid-West of America was in the Mid-West of America seemed watertight. But there were problems in devising a fair system. There were some noble attempts to solve the problem, but somehow they did not ring true for England, let alone Wales. When the Centre of Policy Studies came up with specific, national tests for 7-year-olds the questions they suggested[21] did not carry the nation with them—but things are beginning to change. Maths should be questions like

1. Answer, without paper, 9 + 8

2. Calculate, without carrying, 942 + 121

3. Calculate, with carrying, 44 - 26

4. Tell time to nearest hour

5. Start learning tables

In English, they should, for example, be able to write legibly, use a wide range of simple vocabulary, construct sentences in simple syntax, using full stops and capital letters correctly, spell words correctly, know by heart some simple poems like 'I had a little nut tree'.

What, then, of the alleged breakdown of the alleged consensus? There has been a political confrontation, certainly, but less between the political parties than between central government and local government over control of the system. If there had been a consensus here after the war, and based on the Welsh evidence this is highly dubious, it certainly has broken down. And it was this reassertion of central control, orchestrated by the politicians and executed by the civil servants at the Department of Education and Science (DES), who were just as anxious to see central authority reasserted, which has turned out to be of the greatest significance for Wales.

Maclure[22] argues that 'Between 1976 and 1985—between the Ruskin speech and *Better Schools*, Sir Keith Joseph's White Paper issued in March 1985—the DES worked through the agenda' laid out in the Ruskin College speech. From a Welsh point of view this reassertion of power at the centre was of enormous import because it was accompanied by a greater degree of devolution of power to the Welsh Office than had ever previously been the case. As a result of the convergence of these two trends there was potentially greater control of education in Wales from within Wales than ever before. And if the DES was, in the 1970s, an 'ambitious bureaucracy', so was the Welsh Office. Successive Secretaries of State for Wales, especially recently, have not been slow to assert their leadership and control in Wales. And they are responsible for education in Wales. In Maclure's words, the 1988 Act 'increased the powers of the Secretary of State for Education and Science (and, where appropriate, the Secretary of State for Wales)'.[23] Appropriateness leaves a lot to fight for.

It has taken many forms. Policy statements for 'England and Wales' are now followed up by policy statements for Wales. For example, when the National Curriculum statement[24] emerged from the DES in July 1987 it was followed by a booklet on the National Curriculum in Wales.[25] So, if we do not have the independence founded in law of Scotland, we do have some basic elements of the Scottish system which serve to distinguish it. The elements in Scotland are the Scottish Education Department, including HMI, the Consultative Committee on the Curriculum and the Scottish Examination Board. In Wales we now have equivalents all along the line, the Welsh Office Education Department (WOED), including a far more homogeneous group of HMI than is the case in England, the Curriculum Council for Wales (CCW) and the Welsh Joint Education Committee (WJEC). There are also in Wales the equivalent advantages of small size and greater community of purpose. In Scotland we read that 'members of HMI...have traditionally played a key role in the design, implementation and evaluation of all recent major curriculum initiatives...the SED, through HMI, has played a dominant role on all the major committees and working parties responsible for curriculum design and development in Scotland'.[26]

In the new centralist climate of control we must look to the Welsh HMI and the WOED to play the equivalent role in Wales. This does not allow for any diminution in the size of the Welsh inspectorate. As is happening in Scotland, its numbers must expand to fulfil this role adequately.

The framework for the separate administration of education in Wales is now complete. For the first time ever, and we go back to battles fought in the period before World War I, it is intended that Welsh education from nursery to university will be in the hands of the Welsh Office. When the National [sic] Curriculum Council was set up for England it was complemented by the Curriculum Council for Wales. So, the infrastructure in Wales complements the growing responsibilities of political masters in an increasingly centralized education system. Then there has been the practical input on the curriculum, and here we see the realities of Welsh autonomy. On the one prong of the 1988 Act, the devolution of power to schools, there was, and is, no way in which Wales was going to be exempted from the system. On the other, the National Curriculum, the Welsh Office had everything to fight for and, supported from below, it did fight. Given that there is a National Curriculum, Wales has emerged reasonably well, again by being able to get on with the proper job and not being enmeshed in media hysterics. The prime example of this, of course, is the History element of the National Curriculum.

The problem then has been, and to some extent still is, that of defining the Welsh education which we expect these central authorities to implement. By implication there is nothing distinctively Welsh about the theory of the operation of competition between schools, although some in Wales might want to argue that it is less in harmony with our community traditions. The other practical point is that it is irrelevant over most of Wales. We are a rural country, and the free market for those parents without a helicopter who want to see something of their children in their formative years does not actually allow much choice of school. Fortunately, it is what has become centralized that is of the essence to Wales—what is actually taught in the curriculum. That is why, ultimately, the 1988 Act is of such crucial importance in the history of education in Wales.

THE LANGUAGE DEBATE

I have, so far, tried to argue that the Ruskin speech and what has happened since, have inadvertently raised questions about the Welshness of education and made possible a liberating degree of independence in implementing it. You may well respond that there have been debates in Wales which have no English counterpart and we ought to concentrate our minds on those. Paradoxically, I would argue that exclusive concentration on these would be dangerous. I wish to raise, very superficially, the issue of Welsh-language education.

Colin Baker has called this the 'gentle revolution'.[27] One designated bilingual secondary school in 1945, 18 in 1988. Welsh is now taught as a first language in 64 secondary schools in Wales. Baker also claims that 'the formal subject curriculum, the pastoral curriculum, and not least the hidden curriculum have become progressively more Welsh since 1956'.[28] For many years it was deemed appropriate to teach science and mathematics through the medium of English but that too has changed. The numbers of schools using Welsh for teaching Mathematics, Technology, PE, Physics and Chemistry are all up. In 1963 there were 90 entries through the medium of Welsh at O-Level. In 1987 there were 6526 such GCSE entries. This is significant because O-Level entries, as they then were, are a measure of the currency of Welsh—its market value.

Such progress has only been possible because of official support—and it has grown steadily. Contrary to much propaganda, the Welsh language has not lacked for state approval and it has certainly not lacked backing over the decades from HMI, since the first chief inspector, O.M. Edwards, set the tone after 1907. What has happened since the war is that this support has meshed with parental support and pressure to an extent unthinkable between the wars. For all those of us who believe in the importance of the Welsh language here has been a real success story. It has been reinforced now by the inclusion of Welsh as a core or foundation subject in the National Curriculum.

Not that we should be lulled into complacency. Any historical analysis shows how fragile the situation is. The population of Wales is over 80 per cent English-monolingual, and just under 20 per cent English/Welsh bilingual. Virtually everyone in Wales now is open to the educational and conditioning influences of the mass media. Nine miles outside Aberystwyth I drive past a small farmhouse near the village of Llanrhystud on the coast of west Wales, historically the least penetrable by outside influences. I see a satellite dish pointing skywards. An Australian has brought American English to Llanrhystud. In the age group 3 to 14, nearly 146,000 children spoke Welsh in 1901; in 1971, 69,350. Great efforts are still required if the language is to be safeguarded.

To give just one example of the kind of effort needed, education research into bilingualism has played a relatively small part in the revival. This contrasts significantly with Canada, for example, where research has shown the advantages of balanced bilingualism and strongly influenced Canadian parents' views on bilingualism. The same should apply in Wales.

But concentrating on Welsh-language education is dangerous. Because it is so important it has tended to monopolize interest in Wales. It is all too easy to slip into arguing that a Welsh education is an education in the Welsh language. The majority of the Welsh do not speak the language, however much we hope that number may increase. The majority of the Welsh who speak English have their right to an education which is distinctively Welsh.

THE OUTCOME OF THE GREAT DEBATE IN WALES

May I then try to sum up my own views as to where Wales stands in relation to some of the issues raised in the Great Debate and the revolution which has followed it?

First, I have argued that we are not hamstrung by the dogma of such bodies as the Centre for Policy Studies. There were no Welsh contributors to the Black Papers. There has been no anti-teacher hysteria in Wales.

Secondly, there has been no outcry against child-centred excesses in the primary school, because there is no evidence that there have been any. It is inconceivable that, if there had been, the media would have refrained from reporting them. The evidence is that Welsh primary schools have been 'traditional', devoting their long mornings to the 3 'R's and their shorter afternoons to the rest of the curriculum.

Thirdly, there has been none of the backlash against the General Certificate of Secondary Education (GCSE) *per se* that was evident in England. The recent major survey of all History, Geography and Welsh at that level[29] indicated that teachers of the three subjects, without exception, backed the change.

Fourthly, we have a practical situation which is more conducive to a common purpose in Wales. We have a country of state comprehensive schools which are now of more manageable size than they used to be, much more capable of forging a common sense of community, far less prone to large-scale opting out. We have no private sector of any great significance in Wales.

Fifthly, we have a Welsh curriculum. The essential prerequisite of this was a National Curriculum, but then it was necessary for there to be sufficient of a will in the Welsh Office and a sufficiently well-developed curriculum theory and voice, to press for separate treatment for Wales. We have got that in the language, the history and the geography of the nation. That is by far the most critical achievement. It remains now to ensure that a Welsh dimension should permeate the curriculum, as a cross-curricular dimension, taking in, additionally, other subjects such as music and art and Anglo-Welsh literature. Mediating this to schools seems to me to be a major responsibility of the Curriculum Council for Wales, one which they have been addressing already.

Sixthly, we have an institutional framework. The Welsh Office now has a degree of influence over Welsh education which would have been unthinkable thirty years ago. There is an interesting historical perspective here. In a time of strong cultural nationalism, in the last decade of the nineteenth century and the first of the twentieth, Wales was nearly granted a National Council for Education. What it received from Lloyd George was the Welsh Department of the Board of Education. There is a famous story[30] of how its first Permanent Secretary, Alfred Davies, asked the 'English' Permanent Secretary, Morant, for some Board of Education headed notepaper just before he assumed office. He received a crushing rebuke which would have destroyed many a more thin-skinned Welshman. Over the next decades Davies asked for more than notepaper. Not from any Welsh perspective, but from insatiable personal ambition, he was to call for Welsh Department control over technical education, special needs education, as we would call it now, the school health service, and control of university education. He was fought tooth and nail by senior English civil servants. Now, for the first time ever, we have the near prospect of Welsh Office administration of all aspects of Welsh education, including financing higher education through a separate funding council. The symbolic significance of this is crucial. Its practical import is that it is now up to pressure groups in Wales to help influence the measures which they think ought to reflect the distinctiveness of Wales. In practice, we are now nearer Scotland.

Seventhly, I am not arguing for increased Welsh control of education just as some statement of cultural nationalism. I believe that some of the inherent dangers in the 1988 system need be far less evident in Wales. For example, the CCW is in a position to fight for a curriculum in Wales which is more balanced, as reflected in its position over art and music, or less assessment dominated, in which subjects are not reduced to meeting attainment targets. From a Welsh standpoint, cultural transmission is what is vital, while on a practical basis assessment tables to allow parents to make 'rational' choices are just not required over large tracts of Wales.

Eighthly, on the curriculum, sufficient battles have been won to allow us to talk of a curriculum for Wales, not just a curriculum in Welsh. Whatever we may think of the National Curriculum it is for me, at least, more acceptable as such. There has been goodwill in some unexpected places over the inclusion of Welsh at all key stages as a core or foundation subject, despite the problem of supplying the teachers to implement it. It is good to know that the statutory orders for history[31] in Wales have been at least as well received as those for England. There will now be an organic growth as that which was unforeseen becomes the norm, the frame of reference for future debate. Treating Wales as an educational unit is not only recognition of a different heritage, partly expressed in our educational system, but the path to pragmatic advantages. The linguistic, cultural and organizational differences in education in Wales, if allowed to develop, can shed light on the wider picture in the rest of Britain and in Europe. If and when the teachers of Wales, or the CCW, or the research processes come up with more sense in Wales than in England that good sense ought to be allowed to prevail.

THE NEED FOR CO-ORDINATION

Finally, the only way to achieve the kind of integration of effort which is so desirable in Wales is for the present activities to be co-ordinated. How? Wales is full of educational bodies but often the one is not sufficiently aware of what the other is doing. If we think of the varying briefs and overlapping activities of the schools, the university colleges, the institutes of higher education, Pwyllgor Datblygu Addysg Gymraeg (PDAG), CCW, the WJEC, and the local education authorities (LEAs) we get some idea of the opportunity for crossed wires and unco-ordinated initiatives.

The main paymaster, directly or indirectly, is going to be the Welsh Office. It might seem appropriate that from there, from the civil servants and HMI, should come the co-ordination. In practice, this happens to some extent already. But the Welsh Office is in an invidious position, having to interpret policy laid down for England in a Welsh context and ensuring that more local initiatives from bodies which it funds are, on the one hand not stifled, but on the other not incompatible with wider policies. Not surprisingly the Welsh Office has usually to be reactive not pro-active. I come inexorably to the conclusion that there has to be some co-ordinating body which has a wider role and a wider remit. I have indicated that in the first decade of this century Wales came close to being granted its own National Council for Education, which would have been a large elected body. An elected body would, at least at present, seem politically unacceptable. In these days an Education Council for Wales would be nominated. Such a body, providing an overview of the whole of education, could be of inestimable value in providing for Wales almost as significant a voice in education as has Scotland. And it would need to be supported by the professional expertise not of a diminished band of HMI, but an expanded group, just as is happening in Scotland now. Of course the Education Council for Wales would have to work within the parameters laid down by two Secretaries of State. But within those parameters it would initiate as well as co-ordinate policy and field ideas from individuals and institutions in Wales which would lead to worthwhile practical results. In my view the Curriculum Council for Wales provides the nucleus of such a body and I believe its remit should be extended accordingly.

It was not the intention of the Ruskin College speech to focus attention on Welsh education. On the surface it had no Welsh dimension. But insofar as it has had an impact on later events and legislation, whatever may be the merits and demerits of that legislation on other grounds, I believe that the Welsh have cause to be grateful to a politician who, by interesting irony, waited until his retirement to serve Welsh education by other means.

But I hope that Lord Callaghan will, in the context of this lecture, allow a lady whose sentiments provide me with some cheer in these surrealistic days, to have the last word. On the occasion of a confrontation between Wales and England in educational policy in 1932 she said, on behalf of the Women's Liberal Federation: 'We feel it hard that Wales...should be held back by the more backward English.'[32]

NOTES

1. Bennet, J. (ed.) (1761) *The English Works of Roger Ascham, Preceptor to Queen Elizabeth.* London: no imprint.
2. *Ibid.,* p. 191.
3. *Ibid.,* pp. 191, 192.
4. *Ibid.,* p. 192.
5. Moon, B. (ed.) (1990) *New Curriculum—National Curriculum.* London: Hodder & Stoughton.
6. MacNeil, C. (1990) 'The National Curriculum: A Black Perspective', in Moon, B. op. cit.
7. *Ibid.,* p. 81.
8. Central Advisory Council for Education (England) (1967) *Children and their Primary Schools* (The Plowden Report). London: HMSO.
9. Cox, C.B. and Dyson A.E. (1971) *The Black Papers on Education.* London: Davis-Poynter; originally published, London: Critical Quarterly Society, 1969.
10. Bennett, N. (1976) *Teaching Styles and Pupil Progress.* London: Open Books.
11. See Richards, C. (ed.) (1982) *New Directions in Primary Education.* p. 16.
12. See note 8.
13. Central Advisory Council (Wales) (1949) *The Future of Secondary Education in Wales.* London: HMSO.
14. HMI (Wales) (1991) *Review of Educational Provision in Wales, 1989-90.* Cardiff: Welsh Office.
15. HMI (Wales) (1984) *Curriculum and Organisation of Primary Schools in Wales.* Cardiff: Welsh Office.
16. Ibid. pp. 7, 8.
17. Central Advisory Council for Education (Wales) (1967) *Primary Education in Wales* (The Gittins Report). Cardiff: HMSO.
18. Boyson, R. (1975) *The Crisis in Education.* London: Woburn Press.
19. See Richards, C., op. cit., p. 11.
20. *The Observer,* December 1987.
21. Lawlor, S. (1988) *The Correct Core.* London: Centre for Policy Studies; also published under 'How clever is your child?' *Sunday Mirror,* 23 October 1988.
22. Maclure, S. (1989) *Education Reformed,* 2nd edn. London: Hodder & Stoughton.
23. *Ibid.,* p. v.
24. DES/WO (1987) *The National Curriculum 5-16: A Consultation Document.* London/Cardiff: HMSO.
25. Welsh Office (1987) *The National Curriculum in Wales.* Cardiff: HMSO.
26. Rand, J. (1990) 'A Scottish Tradition of Curricular Reform', in Moon, B., op. cit.
27. Barker, C. (1990) 'The Growth of Bilingual Education in the Secondary Schools of Wales' in Evans, W.G. (ed.) *Perspectives on a Century of Secondary Education in Wales.* Aberystwyth: Centre for Educational Studies.
28. *Ibid.,* p. 83.
29. Daugherty, R., Thomas, B., Jones, G.E. and Davies, S. (1991) *GCSE in Wales.* Cardiff: Welsh Office Education Department.
30. Public Record Office Ed 24/581. See also Jones, G.E. (1982) *Controls and Conflicts in Welsh Secondary Education 1889-1944.* Cardiff: University of Wales Press.
31. Welsh Office (1991) *History in the National Curriculum (Wales).* Cardiff: Welsh Office.
32. Quoted in Simon, B. (1974) *The Politics of Educational Reform 1920-1940.* London: Lawrence & Wishart.

References

ACOST (1991) *Science and Technology: Education and Employment.* London: Advisory Council on Science and Technology.

Alexander, R. (1991) *Primary Education in Leeds.* Leeds: Leeds University School of Education.

Anderson, B. and Karrquist, C. (1983) 'How Swedish pupils aged 12–15 years understand light and its properties', *European Journal of Science Education,* 5, pp. 387–402.

Ashdown, R., Carpenter, B. and Bovair, K. (eds.) (1991) *The Curriculum Challenge: Access to the National Curriculum for Pupils with Severe and Complex Learning Difficulties.* London: Fulton.

Assessment of Performance Unit (1986) *Speaking and Listening.* Windsor: NFER/Nelson.

Barker, C. (1990) 'The Growth of Bilingual Education in the Secondary Schools of Wales', in Evans, W.G. (ed.) *Perspectives on a Century of Secondary Education in Wales.* Aberystwyth: Centre for Educational Studies.

Barnett, C. (1986) *The Audit of War: The Illusion and Reality of Britain as a Great Nation.* London: Macmillan.

Bennet, J. (ed.) (1761) *The English Works of Roger Ascham, Preceptor to Queen Elizabeth.* London: no imprint.

Bennett, N. (1976) *Teaching Styles and Pupil Progress.* London: Open Books.

Bennett, N. and Carré, C. (1993) *Learning to Teach.* London: Routledge.

Bennett, N., Desforges, C., Cockburn, A. and Wilkinson, B. (1984) *The Quality of Pupil Learning Experiences.* London: Erlbaum.

Bennett, N. and Dunne, E. (1992) *Managing Classroom Groups.* Hemel Hempstead: Simon & Schuster.

Bennett, S.N., Wragg, E.C., Carré, C.G. and Carter, D.S.G. (1992) 'A longitudinal study of primary teachers' perceived competence in, and concerns about, National Curriculum implementation', *Research Papers in Education,* 6, (forthcoming).

Boyson, R. (1975) *The Crisis in Education.* London: Woburn Press.

Bradshaw, J. (1990) *Child Poverty and Deprivation in the UK.* London: National Children's Bureau.

Bronfenbrenner, U. (1974) *Is Early Intervention Effective?* Washington, DC: US Department of Health and Welfare.

Bruner, J. and Haste, H. (1987) *Making Sense: The Child's Construction of the World.* London: Methuen.

Cassels, J. (1990) *Britain's Real Skills Shortage.* London: Policy Studies Institute.

Callaghan, J. (1987) *Time and Chance.* London: Collins.

Callaghan, J. (1976) 'Towards a national debate', reprinted in *Education,* 22 October 1976, pp. 332–3.

Central Advisory Council (Wales) (1949) *The Future of Secondary Education in Wales.* London: HMSO.
Central Advisory Council for Education (England) (1967) *Children and their Primary Schools* (The Plowden Report). London: HMSO.
Central Advisory Council for Education (Wales) (1967) *Primary Education in Wales* (The Gittins Report). Cardiff: HMSO.
Commission on Future of Community College Staff (1988) *Building Communities: A Vision for a New Century.* Washington: American Association of Community & Junior Colleges.
Cox, C.B. and Dyson, A.E. (1971) *The Black Papers on Education.* London: Davis-Poynter; originally published, London: Critical Quarterly Society, 1969.
Cox, C.B. and Dyson, A. E. (eds.) (1975) *Black Paper 1975 —The Fight for Education.* London: Dent.

Daugherty, R., Thomas, B., Jones, G.E. and Davies, S. (1991) *GCSE in Wales.* Cardiff: Welsh Office Education Department.
Davie, R., Butler, N. and Goldstein, H. (1972) *From Birth to Seven.* London: Longman.
Department of Education and Science (1975) *A Language for Life* (The Bullock Report). London: HMSO.
Department of Education and Science (1977) *Educating our Children: Four Subjects for Debate.* London: DES.
Department of Education and Science (1978) *Report of the Committee of Enquiry into the Education of Handicapped Children and Young People: Special Educational Needs* (The Warnock Report). London: HMSO.
Department of Education and Science (1979) *Aspects of Secondary Education in England.* London: HMSO.
Department of Education and Science (1980) *A Framework for the School Curriculum.* London: DES.
Department of Education and Science (1982) *A Report of the Committee of Enquiry into the Teaching of Mathematics in Schools in England and Wales, Mathematics Counts* (The Cockcroft Report). London: HMSO.
Department of Education and Science (1985) *Better Schools,* White Paper. London: HMSO.
Department of Education and Science (1985) *Report of the Committee of Enquiry into the Education of Children of Ethnic Minority Groups. Education for All* (The Swann Report). London: HMSO.
Department of Education and Science (1991) *Standards in Education: The Annual Report of HM Senior Chief Inspector of Schools,* 1989–90. London: HMSO.
Department of Education and Science/HMI (1977) *Curriculum 11–16: Working Papers by HM Inspectorate. A Contribution to Current Debate.* London: HMSO.
Department of Education and Science/HMI (1978) *Primary Education in England: A Survey by HMI.* London: HMSO.
Department of Education and Science/HMI (1981) *Curriculum 11–16: A Review of Progress.* London: HMSO.
Department of Education and Science/HMI (1983) *Curriculum 11–16: Towards a Statement of Entitlement: Curricular Reappraisal in Action.* London: HMSO.
Department of Education and Science/HMI (1985) *The Curriculum from 5 to 16.* London: HMSO.
Department of Education and Science/HMI (1989) *Aspects of Primary Education: The Teaching of Mathematics.* London: HMSO.
Department of Education and Science/HMI (1989) *The Lower Attaining Pupils Programme.* London: HMSO.
Department of Education and Science/WO (1987) *Report of the Task Group on Assessment and Testing.* London/Cardiff: HMSO.
Department of Education and Science/WO (1987) *The National Curriculum 5–16: A Consultation Document.* London/Cardiff: HMSO.
Department of Education and Science/WO (1988) *Advancing A Levels* (The Higginson Report). London/Cardiff: HMSO.
Department of Education and Science/WO (1989) *Committee of Enquiry into Discipline in Schools* (The Elton Report). London/Cardiff: HMSO.
Department of Education and Science/WO (1989) *National Curriculum —English for Ages 5 to 11.*

London/Cardiff: HMSO.

Department of Education and Science/WO (1991) *Education and Training for the 21st Century*. London/Cardiff: HMSO.

DHSS (1976) *Fit for the Future* (Report of the Court Committee on Child Health Services). London: HMSO.

Drucker, P. (1989) *The New Realities*. London: Heinemann.

Essen, J. and Wedge, P. (1982) *Continuities in Childhood Disadvantage*. London: Heinemann.

Fagg, S., Aherne, P., Skelton, S. and Thornber, A. (1990) *Entitlement for All in Practice: A Broad, Balanced and Relevant Curriculum for Pupils with Severe and Complex Learning Difficulties*. London: Fulton.

Finegold, D., Keep, E., Miliband, D., Raffe, D., Spours, K. and Young, M. (1990) *A British Baccalaureat*. London: Institute for Public Policy Research.

Fogelman, K. (1983) *Growing Up in Great Britain*. London: Macmillan and National Children's Bureau.

Galton, M., Simon, B. and Croll, P. (1980) *Inside the Primary Classroom*. London: Routledge & Kegan Paul.

Green, J.R. (1989) *Primary Children's Ideas in Science and Teaching Strategies to Develop Scientific Thinking*. M.Ed. dissertation, University of Exeter.

Halsey, A.H. (1972) *Educational Priority*. London: HMSO.

Halsey, A.H. (1972) *Educational Disadvantage*. London: HMSO.

Haywood, C., Begab, M. and Richardson, S. (eds.) (1981) *Psycho-social Aspects of Retarded Performance*. Baltimore, Md.: University Park Press.

Higginson Committee (1988) *Advancing A Levels*. London: HMSO.

HMI (Wales) (1984) *Curriculum and Organisation of Primary Schools in Wales*. Cardiff: Welsh Office.

HMI (Wales) (1991) *Review of Educational Provision in Wales, 1989-90*. Cardiff: Welsh Office.

Hollis, M. (1988) 'Atomic Energy and Moral Glue'. Unpublished paper given at a conference, *The Philosopher's Eye*, organized by Cheshire LEA, Warwick University Institute of Education and The Royal Institute of Philosophy, 15 October 1988.

House of Commons (1986) *Achievement in Primary Schools*, Report of Select Committee on Education, Science and the Arts. London: HMSO.

Hoskins, W.G. (1950) 'The Deserted Villages of Leicestershire', in *Essays in Leicestershire History*. Liverpool: Liverpool University Press.

Hurd, D. (1988) *The New Statesman*, 27 April 1988.

ILEA (1984) *Improving Secondary Education* (The Hargreaves Report). London: ILEA.

ILEA (1985) *Equal Opportunities for All?* (The Fish Report). London: ILEA.

Institute of Manpower Studies (1984) *Competence and Competition: Training and Education in the Federal Republic of Germany, the United States and Japan*. London: NEDO

Kruger, C. and Summers, M. (1989) 'An investigation of some primary teachers' understandings of changes in materials', *School Science Review*, 71, pp. 17–27.

Lake, R. (1991) 'Reading Standards in Buckinghamshire Primary Schools'. Unpublished report, Bucks County Council.

Lawlor, S. (1988) *The Correct Core*, London: Centre for Policy Studies; also published under 'How clever is your child?' *Sunday Mirror*, 23 October 1988.

Maclure, S. (1989) *Education Reformed*, 2nd edn. London: Hodder & Stoughton.

MacNeil, C.(1990) 'The National Curriculum: A Black Perspective', in Moon, B. (ed.) *New Curriculum*

—*National Curriculum*. London: Hodder & Stoughton.

Marshall, C. (1991) 'Culture Change', *RSA Journal*, CXXXIX/5414, 1991.

Miliband, D. (1991) *Markets, Politics and Education: Beyond the Education Reform Act*. London: Institute for Public Policy Research.

Mittler, P. (1989) 'Warnock and Swann: Similarities and Differences', in Verma, G.(ed.) *Education for All: A Landmark in Pluralism*. London: Falmer.

Moon, B. (ed.) (1990) *New Curriculum—National Curriculum*. London: Hodder & Stoughton.

Mortimore, P., Sammons, P., Ecob, R. and Stoll, L. (1988) *School Matters: The Junior Schools*. Salisbury: Open Books.

Moser, C. (1990) *Our Need for an Informed Society*. Presidential Address, British Association, London.

National Youth Employment Council (1974) *The Unqualified, Untrained and Unemployed*. London: HMSO.

NCC (1991) *Guidance and INSET Materials for Pupils with Severe Learning Difficulties*, York: NCC.

Neave, G. (1988) 'Education and Social Policy: Demise of an Ethic or Change of Values ?', *Oxford Review of Education*, 14 (3).

OECD (1975) *Educational Development Strategy in England and Wales*. Paris: OECD.

Pilling, D. (1990) *Escape from Disadvantage*. London: Falmer Press.

Public Record Office Ed 24/581. See also Jones, G.E. (1982) *Controls and Conflicts in Welsh Secondary Education 1889–1944*. Cardiff: University of Wales Press.

Rand, J. (1990) 'A Scottish Tradition of Curricular Reform', in Moon, B. (ed.) *New Curriculum—National Curriculum*. London: Hodder & Stoughton.

Resnick, L.B. (1989) 'Cognitive Apprenticeships' in Resnick, L.B. (ed.) *Knowing, Learning and Instruction: Essays in Honor of Robert Glaser*. Hillsdale, NJ: Erlbaum.

Richards, C. (ed.) (1982) *New Directions in Primary Education*. Falmer: London.

RSA (1991) *Education for Capability: The Campaign*. London: Royal Society of Arts.

Rutter, M., Maugham, B., Mortimore, P. and Ouston, D. (1979) *Fifteen Thousand Hours: Secondary Schools and their Effects on Children*. London: Open Books.

Sacks, J. (1990) 'The Reith Lectures for 1990', *The Listener*, 6 December 1990, p. 17.

Sainsbury, D. (1990) *Education for Wealth Creation*. London: TSB Group plc.

Schools Inquiry Commission (1868) *The Taunton Commission*. London: HMSO.

School Examinations and Assessment Council (1991) *APU Mathematics Monitoring 1984–88 (Phase 2)*. Slough: NFER.

Simon, B. (1974) *The Politics of Educational Reform 1920–1940*. London: Lawrence & Wishart.

Smith, D. and Tomlinson, S. (1989) *The School Effect: A Study of Multi-Racial Comprehensives*. London: Policy Studies Institute.

Southgate, V., Arnold, H. and Johnson, S. (1981) *Extending Beginning Reading*. London: Heinemann.

Stradling, P. and Saunders, H. (1991) *The Lower Attaining Pupils Programme: An Evaluation*. Windsor: NFER/Nelson.

Swann, W. (1991) *Integration Statistics*. London: Centre for Studies in Integrated Education.

Toffler, A. (1970) *Future Shock*. London: Bodley Head.

Tomlinson, J. (1986) 'Public Education, Public Good', *Oxford Review of Education*, 12 (3).

Topping, K. and Wolfendale, S. (1985) *Parental Involvement in Children's Reading*. London: Croom Helm.

Townsend, P. and Whitehead, N. (1988) *Inequalities in Health*. London: Penguin.

Townsend, P. (1991) *The Poor are Poorer: A Statistical Report on Changing Living Standards of Rich and Poor in the United Kingdom 1979–1988*. Bristol University: Department of Social Policy and Planning.

Vygotsky, L.S. (1962) *Thought and Language*. Cambridge, Mass.: MIT Press.

Vygotsky, L.S. (1978) *Mind in Society: The Development of Higher Psychological Processes*. Cambridge, Mass.: Harvard University Press.

Wedge, P. and Prosser, H. (1973) *Born to Fail?* London: Arrow Books and National Children's Bureau.

Welsh Office (1987) *The National Curriculum in Wales*. Cardiff: HMSO.

Welsh Office (1991) *History in the National Curriculum (Wales)*. Cardiff: Welsh Office.

Widlake, P. (1985) *Reducing Educational Disadvantage*. London: Routledge & Kegan Paul.

Wiener, M.J. (1981) *English Culture and the Decline of the Industrial Spirit, 1850-1980*. Cambridge: Cambridge University Press.

Wragg, E.C. (1980) 'State-approved knowledge ? Ten steps down the slippery slope', in Golby, M. (ed.) *The Core Curriculum* (Perspectives, 2). Exeter: University of Exeter.

Wragg, E.C., Bennett, S.N. and Carré, C.G. (1989) 'Primary teachers and the National Curriculum', *Research Papers in Education*, 4, pp. 17–37.

Zuboff, S. (1988) *The Age of the Smart Machine: The Future of Work and Power*. New York: Basic Books.

Index